Letts EXPLORE

D0525243

World War One Poetry

Guide written by

Ron Simpson

A *Letts* Literature Guide

First published 1997

Letts Educational
Aldine House
Aldine Place
London W12 8AW
0181 740 2266

Text © Ron Simpson 1997

Typeset by Jordan Publishing Design

Text design Jonathan Barnard

Cover and text illustrations Hugh Marshall

Graphic illustration Hugh Marshall

Design © BPP (Letts Educational) Ltd

British Library Cataloguing in Publication Data
A CIP record for this book is available from the British Library

ISBN 1 85758 495 3

Printed and bound in Great Britain
by Nuffield Press, Abingdon

Letts Educational is the trading name of BPP (Letts Educational) Ltd

Contents

What did you do

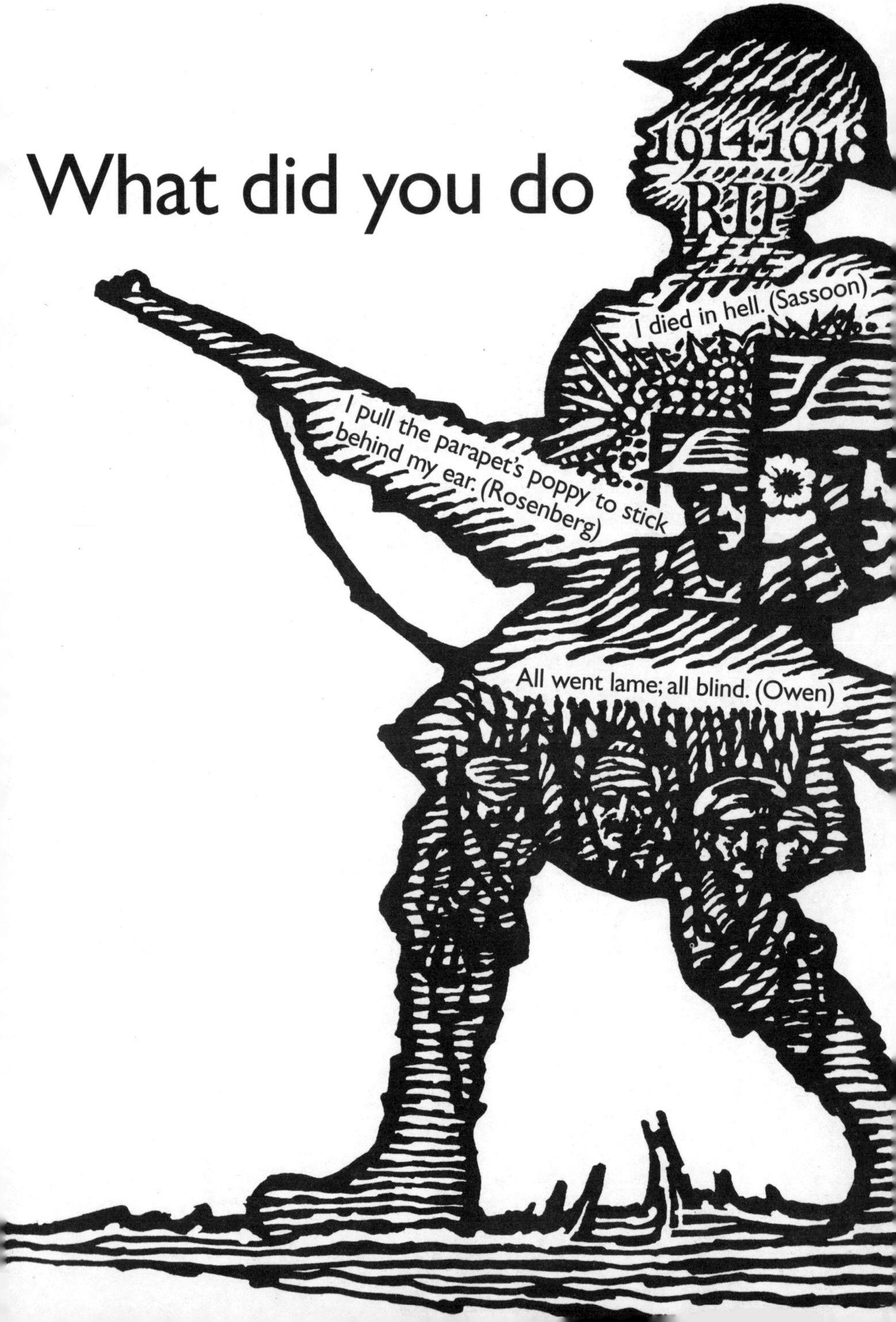

in the Great War?

Forever England. (Brooke)

This tumult in the clouds. (Yeats)

Never such innocence again. (Larkin)

■ The impact of the Great War

The First World War was known at the time as the Great War, and so it was. No previous war had the same impact in terms of crusading zeal, widespread disillusionment, loss of life or social change. But our concern in this Literature · Guide is with the fact that the Great War produced more remarkable poetry *by poets involved as fighting men* than any other conflict.

Why should this be? To begin with, the idea of a noble cause inspired many to verse, and many more to volunteer. When these volunteers were subject to slaughter on a scale never before seen (57,000 men were killed on the first *day* of the Battle of the Somme) and the survivors had to endure an apparently endless campaign, the poetry of passion, pity and satire emerged.

The Great War was never supposed to last: 'over by Christmas' was the slogan. Since the end of the Napoleonic Wars a century before, all Britain's wars had been far distant, involved comparatively few troops (mostly regulars) and were often fought against sadly ill-equipped foes. This was the first major European war fought with modern military technology: machine guns, huge artillery pieces and gas, and later, tanks and aeroplanes. And all this was just over the Channel: although there were many theatres of war, the focus of attention was the Western Front, sweeping through Belgium and across Northern France.

The strange mixture of despair, humour and comradeship among the soldiers was based partly on the fact that only they knew what the war was like. For many civilians in Britain, there was nothing like the suffering which was to come in World War Two, though there were some zeppelin (airship) raids to worry about. The soldiers wrote about the war constantly. Their songs still move us to anger, pity and amusement, as in the 1960s musical show and film, *Oh, What a Lovely War!* Books and plays based on war experiences appeared throughout the 1920s. In *Goodbye to All That*, the autobiography of poet Robert Graves, he writes of going on leave to London and feeling out of place (and furiously angry) among people who talked about war, but continued their social lives. Above all, though, the Great War is remembered in literature for the poetry of serving soldiers (often young junior officers), many of whom failed to survive.

■ Who's who: the poets

The poets of the First World War were far too numerous to attempt an account of all of them. They included professional writers, established poets and aspiring poets whose writings were transformed by war. They also included ordinary soldiers, moved by the scenes they witnessed, and such unexpected figures as 'Woodbine Willie' – an army chaplain, Rev. G.A. Studdert Kennedy, whose morale-boosting rhymes were very popular. Here we concentrate on six of the most important, plus the last of the war poets.

Rupert Brooke (1887–1915)

Rupert Brooke was widely regarded as one of the most promising poets, and one of the most brilliant young men, of the pre-war period. He was among the most prominent of the 'Georgian' poets (George V had come to the throne in 1910) and his first volume of poetry was published in 1911. Brooke is one of the few war poets whose pre-war poems are also highly regarded. *The Old Vicarage, Grantchester,* for instance, is still popular and contains two lines which sum up the cosy security of the pre-war world:

> 'Stands the church clock at ten to three?
> And is there honey still for tea?'

Rupert Brooke's war poetry is full of the optimistic patriotism of the first months of the Great War. He himself saw action briefly with the Royal Naval Division, but died of blood poisoning on the way to Gallipoli early in 1915. His finest and most typical war poem, *The Soldier*, one of his '1914' sonnets, is examined on pages 16-17.

Wilfred Owen (1893–1918)

Wilfred Owen, in many ways, typifies the war poet. Before the war he had lived a rather sheltered existence, working as a private tutor and assistant to a country vicar. He also wrote poetry, attempting the style of the Romantic poet, John Keats. Owen's pre-war poems, full of description and about very little, do not have much to recommend them. The war transformed his poetry, giving it a new power. He enlisted in 1915, was commissioned in 1916, spent two stints at the Front (one of six months), won the Military Cross and was killed a week before the Armistice in 1918.

But, if Owen is the typical 'trench poet', it is a mistake to think of his poems as being scribbled down under fire. He really reached maturity as a poet in the months he spent recuperating at Craiglockhart Hospital near Edinburgh in 1917, where Siegfried Sassoon advised and assisted him. Detailed drafts of his poems show how meticulous he was.

Wilfred Owen summed up his own poetry better than anyone else in the preface he wrote to a volume of his poems, edited by Sassoon and published in 1920:

> 'Above all I am not concerned with Poetry.
> My subject is War, and the pity of War.
> The Poetry is in the pity.'

Poems by Wilfred Owen are analysed in many sections of this book, on pages 16–19, 22–23, 34–35, 42–45, 46–47, 48–51 and 53.

Siegfried Sassoon (1886–1967)

Siegfried Sassoon was the angry satirist among First World War poets. Despite his aristocratic background, he enlisted as a trooper, but soon found himself (like Owen) an officer serving on the Western Front. Also like Owen, he received the Military Cross, was several times severely wounded (the last a head wound in 1918) and spent much of 1917 at Craiglockhart Hospital.

Where Sassoon was unique was that – despite being a serving officer with an awesome reputation for reckless courage – he chose to oppose the war publicly. In 1917, his attack on the war was read in the House of Commons and he threw his Military Cross ribbon into the Mersey. In this he risked treason charges, but Sassoon was one of the survivors of war.

Sassoon dwells less on the pity of war and more on the criminal incompetence of those who were in power. His poems are particularly important in our study of the subject of **The Higher Ranks** (beginning on page 32), but are also analysed on pages 20–21, 24–25, 26–27 and 50–51.

Edward Thomas (1878–1917)

Like so many of the war poets, Edward Thomas served with notable courage as a junior officer on the Western Front and was killed in action. The major difference between Thomas and the other war poets is that he was of an earlier generation. For many years, he had been earning a very precarious living by writing – mainly travel and biography.

Shortly before war broke out, a meeting with the American poet Robert Frost led Thomas to turn to poetry. His poems were mainly realistic evocations of English country life and he wrote few war poems as such. Those he did write are filled with a generous absence of hatred, and a mature vision of what England and peace meant to him.

Poems by Edward Thomas are examined on pages 28–29, 38–39 and 52–54.

Isaac Rosenberg (1890–1918)

Originally apprenticed as an engraver in the East End of London, Isaac Rosenberg had already exhibited paintings and published poetry before war broke out. His Jewish background no doubt helped to give his poetry a sense of international sympathy, but it was mixed with a keen sense of patriotism. In South Africa because of ill health when war was declared, Rosenberg returned to Britain in 1915, enlisted, was sent to France (despite poor health) in 1916 and was killed in action. Despite the praise of such survivors as Laurence Binyon and Siegfried Sassoon, it is only in the last 20 years that Rosenberg has been recognised as one of the great poets of World War One.

In this book we examine two of Isaac Rosenberg's poems of active service: on pages 26–27 and 40–41.

Charles Sorley (1895–1915)

Though not so widely known as other victims of the war, such as Rupert Brooke or Wilfred Owen, Charles Sorley perhaps sums up most completely the waste of a generation of young men. In 1914 he left his school, Marlborough College, with a place at Oxford University waiting for him. He spent the summer in (of all places) Germany, returned when war broke out, joined up and was dead before the end of 1915.

Two of Charles Sorley's small body of poems are examined on pages 36–37 and 46–47.

Geoffrey Dearmer (1893–1996)

Astonishingly, the last of the war poets died while this book was being written: in August 1996. In later years, Geoffrey Dearmer spent 20 years as editor of BBC radio's *Children's Hour*! His best known poem, *The Turkish Trench Dog*, a reminder that the Germans had their allies too, is examined on pages 40–41.

■ Themes and subjects

Heroism

Heroism and survival

Men frequently spoke of heroes in the Great War. Even politicians used the word: in November 1918, at the end of the war, Lloyd George talked of making Britain 'a fit country for heroes to live in'. But, after the first months of the war, the soldier-poets (who themselves often behaved very bravely, even heroically) had little to do with the concept. Heroes devoted to a noble cause found that much of their time was spent in nerve-jangling squalor and idleness, where heroism seemed inappropriate and survival became the goal. Only those on the Home Front, who knew nothing of war, still spoke of heroism. Wilfred Owen's poem *S.I.W* draws a vivid picture of the draining of heroism and the illusions of those at home.

Patriotism

Patriotism

Patriotism takes many forms. The kind that believes in 'my country right or wrong', and sees foreigners as enemies, did not last among the soldiers of the Great War. At first, there were volunteers who wished to fight for a noble cause, but generally aggressive nationalism belonged to the armchair patriots, those living safely at home. Concepts such as 'it is sweet and honourable to die for one's country' seemed like lies to the soldier-poets, who in many cases were about to do just that. Owen's contempt for Jessie Pope in *Dulce et Decorum est* is typical.

If patriotism means a love of one's country – not aggressive, but based on a regard for what is good – this can be found, notably (but not solely) in the poems of Edward Thomas.

The enemy

The enemy

You are probably familiar with the story of the British and German troops on the Western Front playing football together on Christmas Day, 1914. Although senior officers objected and the game was never repeated, there was a strange feeling of comradeship across 'No Man's Land'. You will find it hard to discover words of hatred for the Germans or their allies in the poems of World War One. Why should this be? Largely because the soldiers on both sides viewed the 'enemy' as victims of the same absurd trick of fate.

So, who was to blame? Who was the enemy? You will not have to read far to identify them as the staff officers, the politicians and the armchair patriots. The soldiers' songs mocked them, imagining them playing leapfrog: 'One Staff Officer jumped right over another Staff Officer's back'. Sassoon's *The General* is stinging, bitter satire of the real enemy. In *The Next War* Owen even writes: 'Death was never an enemy of ours!' and claims that what is wrong is warring on 'men – for flags'.

The victims

The victims

Who were the victims? Those killed in war, obviously, but the war poets found many other victims of the conflict. There were those disabled by wounds: as in the American Civil War, the medical ability of the time was outstripped by the technology of destruction in the Great War. There were mental cases: victims of what was called 'shell shock', gradually broken down by the pressure of daily exposure to death. There were suicides. Above all, though, the victims were all those who suffered from exposure, loss of friends and comrades, and inexplicable orders.

Peace

Peace

Peace takes many forms in the poetry of the First World War. Obviously, the soldiers desired the end of the war: perhaps the best known soldiers' song, a parody of *What a Friend I Have in Jesus*, begins: 'When this lousy war is over' and lists the things he is happy to leave behind. But there are other places to look for peace. Edward Thomas found it in the continuation of ordinary life in *As the Team's Head-Brass*, Isaac Rosenberg managed to feel it on the battlefield in *Returning, We Hear the Larks*, other poems find peace in sleep and dreams – maybe of death.

Poetic techniques

Diction

Diction

The term *diction* refers to the vocabulary of a poem, the sort of words that the poet chooses to use. You should be aware of various types of diction in the poems you are studying:

- **Heroic diction**, very often using abstract words like 'glory' and 'nobility', is not as frequently used as you might expect. There are some examples, however, of its use in early poems and some ironic use of heroic diction by poets such as Siegfried Sassoon and Wilfred Owen.
- **Colloquial diction** means the ordinary words of conversation. You will find this used frequently, both in slang or dialect and in ordinary, simple vocabulary. Although most of the poets were officers, they were not senior officers and most shared the same view of the war as the ordinary soldiers.
- **Biblical language** is a term used for the solemn simplicity often found in World War One poetry.
- **Emotional diction** attempts to convey the sense of shock, pity or anger felt by the poets.

Alliteration

Alliteration and onomatopoeia

Both these techniques are commonly used by poets and are easily linked together, as both deal with the sound of words. *Onomatopoeia* is a difficult Greek word with a very simple meaning: the sound suggests the meaning of the word. There are many ordinary words that are based on onomatopoeia: from 'bang' to 'whisper', from 'tinkle' to 'crash'. It is easy to see how war poetry would make much use of this device. *Alliteration*, on the other hand, refers to repeating a consonant sound, usually at the beginning of words. Some World War One poets (such as Wilfred Owen) sometimes used alliteration almost to excess to convey the drama of the situation.

Satire

Satire

Satire can be very amusing, but the World War One poets inevitably found only a bitter, wry humour in their satirical pieces. The essence of satire is to criticise by humour or mockery and the targets in this case were superior officers, politicians and patriots ignorant of war. Satire is found particularly in the poems of Siegfried Sassoon and is sometimes linked with *irony*. Verbal irony is in some way saying or writing the opposite of the intended meaning, for satirical effect.

Metaphor and simile

Metaphor

Metaphor is at the heart of nearly all poetry. For our purposes, however, it is more convenient to define *simile* first. This is quite simply a comparison, which tells the reader about the thing being described by reference to something else. The comparison is obvious and usually contains the word 'like' or 'as'. You probably already know a poem that begins with a simile about soldiers: '*Like* old beggars under sacks'.

Metaphor does not make the comparison obvious: it is an implied comparison. When, later on in the same poem, the soldiers are said to be '*drunk* with fatigue', we realise that they are not really drunk. You will also encounter a form of metaphor which treats non-humans as though they are persons: *personification*. Death may be personified, or England presented as a 'mother to her people'.

Sonnet

Sonnet

Oddly enough (since the sonnet began as a fifteenth-century Italian love poem), several of the finest Great War poems are written in sonnet form. The *sonnet* is a 14-line poem, usually divided in one of two ways:

octave (eight lines)/**sestet** (six lines)

three **quatrains** (four lines each)/**couplet** (two lines)

There are two main forms of the sonnet, but it must be emphasised that a sonnet *does not need* to fit either of these forms. For reference, though, here are these two forms:

Italian Sonnet: an **octave** rhyming ABBAABBA, and a **sestet** using new rhyme sounds and not ending in a couplet.

Elizabethan Sonnet: three **quatrains** and a **couplet**, using the rhyme scheme ABAB, CDCD, EFEF, GG.

You will find that the sonnets you study do not necessarily use either of these formulas.

Stanza

Throughout this book, the word *stanza* is used for something you might normally call a 'verse'. The word 'verse' has various shifts of meaning, so 'stanza' is used here. It means a section of a poem that is regularly repeated, with the same line lengths, arrangements of rhymes, etc. An irregular division of a poem, for reasons of meaning, is not a stanza.

■ Text commentary

In this commentary on poetry of the First World War, poems are arranged by subject matter and poets' viewpoints, not by poets. Each section consists of between two and six pages, usually dealing with three or four main poems. The poems themselves (with notes, questions and icons) are printed on the left-hand pages, although occasionally it is not possible, because of their length, to print all of every poem in a section. The main commentary is on the right-hand pages, usually opposite the text of the relevant poem, although you will find that occasionally the commentary continues on the next page. To begin with, you should read this brief introduction to **War Poetry of the Nineteenth Century***.*

The tradition of heroism

Whilst we cannot be sure what the serving soldiers and officers wrote for their

Heroism

own relief or pleasure, the war poetry of the nineteenth century, as we know it, is much more 'official' – i.e. written by professional poets who were not there – than the poetry of the First World War. Much of the war poetry was, in fact, written about wars of long ago, like the famous *Horatius* (one of Macaulay's *Lays of Ancient Rome*) about a great hero of classical

times. Perhaps the best-known nineteenth century war poem dealing with contemporary events is *The Charge of the Light Brigade* by Lord Tennyson (1809–92), which serves as a contrast to the poems of Owen, Sassoon and others.

In the Crimean War, at the Battle of Balaclava, a series of mistaken orders sent the Light Brigade on a hopeless charge that caused horrific slaughter. This was the worst example (of many in the war) of the bungling of the British High Command. But what did Tennyson write (second stanza)?

> ' "Forward, the Light Brigade!"
> Was there a man dismay'd?
> Not tho' the sóldier knew
>   Someone had blunder'd:
> Theirs not to make reply,
> Theirs not to reason why,
> Theirs but to do and die:
> Into the Valley of Death
>   Rode the six hundred.'

Patriotism

There is a reference to the mistake, but it is only made by 'someone' and it is a 'blunder', not criminal negligence (or, worse, murder). Instead, the unthinking patriotism of the soldiers is emphasised. After most of the Light Brigade have been slaughtered, the poem ends:

'Honour the charge they made!
Honour the Light Brigade,
Noble six hundred!'

The Light Brigade had indeed acted heroically, but do you think this is the view of events a survivor would have taken? Were the Light Brigade really content 'not to reason why'? In 1854 (when the charge occurred) Tennyson was Poet Laureate, the official poet of Queen and Empire. For what audience was he writing? What effect did he want to make?

You will also notice, if you read the poem in full, that there is no reference to bloodshed except in general terms ('reel'd from the sabre stroke', 'horse and hero fell', and so on). A similarly clean and heroic approach to death comes in *The Burial of Sir John Moore after Corunna* by Charles Wolfe (1791–1823). General Moore fought a highly effective defensive campaign in the Peninsular War (1809), ending with the successful Battle of Corunna, in

Diction

which he was killed. A fine solemnity fills the poem, from the opening lines with a rhythm that supplies the missing drum:

'Not a drum was heard, not a funeral note,
As his corse to the ramparts we hurried.'

corse: corpse, body

The poem is full of words like 'warrior', 'martial', 'fame' and 'glory'. There is also a telling comparison with poems like Rupert Brooke's *The Soldier*, which deal with the British soldier buried in foreign soil. After the battle, the British fleet evacuated the army, with Wolfe hoping the enemy would:

'let him sleep on
In the grave where a Briton has laid him.'

Who was the poet for the ordinary soldier in the nineteenth century? That role went to Rudyard Kipling (1865–1936). Kipling wrote some Great War poems, although there were differences from the World War soldier-poets.

 Kipling wrote mainly of the soldiers of the standing armies, who were considered barely respectable. He dealt mainly with the soldier in India or Africa, not in Europe, and adopted a heavily jokey slang for his *Barrack-Room Ballads*. Above all, Kipling was seen as a poet of the Empire, conscious of British

Patriotism

superiority. But a poem like *Tommy* ('Tommy Atkins', the nickname for the British private soldier) does put the soldiers' point of view:

'For it's Tommy this, an' Tommy that, an' "Chuck him out, the brute!"
But it's "Saviour of 'is country" when the guns begin to shoot.'

Sonnet

The Soldier

If I should die, think only this of me:
　That there's some corner of a foreign field
That is forever England. There shall be
　In that rich earth a richer dust concealed;
A dust whom England bore, shaped, made aware,
　Gave, once, her flowers to love, her ways to roam,
A body of England's, breathing English air,
　Washed by the rivers, blest by suns of home.

And think, this heart, all evil shed away,
　A pulse in the eternal mind, no less
　Gives somewhere back the thoughts by England given;
Her sights and sounds; dreams happy as her day;
　And laughter, learnt of friends; and gentleness,
In hearts at peace, under an English heaven.

Rupert Brooke

Sonnet

Anthem for Doomed Youth

What passing-bells for these who die as cattle?
Only the monstrous anger of the guns.
Only the stuttering rifles' rapid rattle
Can patter out their hasty orisons.
No mockeries now for them; no prayers or bells,
Nor any voice of mourning save the choirs –
The shrill, demented choirs of wailing shells;
And bugles calling for them from sad shires.

What candles may be held to speed them all?
Not in the hands of boys, but in their eyes
Shall shine the holy glimmers of good-byes.
The pallor of girls' brows shall be their pall;
Their flowers the tenderness of patient minds,
And each slow dusk a drawing-down of blinds.

Wilfred Owen

passing bells: the tolling of bells to denote death
orisons: prayers
pall: cloth over coffin

Remembering the dead is, inevitably, a major theme of First World War poetry. Now our main contact with the events of 80 years ago is through Remembrance Day services and war memorials. Ted Hughes, a modern poet, uses the device of an old photograph in *Six Young Men* to lead into memories. But remembering the dead was a theme even in the first days of the war: *For the Fallen* was written only a month after war began and Rupert Brooke's *The Soldier* was also penned in 1914.

The Soldier in many ways sums up the mood of the first months of the war.

Patriotism

Rupert Brooke is happy to die for his country, but knows nothing of what came before death for many soldiers on the Western Front: exposure, mud, the constant dangers of snipers or barrage, the regular loss of friends and comrades. So there is a sort of serenity in the poem, despite the subject matter: even the words '*If* I should die' suggest that he expects to survive. If he is to die, his Englishness will remain: England will somehow colonise that 'foreign field' and even take over heaven!

In this poem Brooke personifies his homeland as 'England' (two examples are marked with *metaphor* icons). Why 'England', not 'Britain'? Try to make a list of all the qualities that Brooke's 'England' possesses in this poem. You will also find another poem in this section which uses 'England' in the same way, though less frequently.

Diction

Though Brooke's view of war was overtaken by events, this remains an effective and moving poem, one of the finest of the opening months of the war. The striking first two and a half lines perfectly express the patriotism of the time. The first line grabs attention by its frankness and the simplicity of the diction (almost all the words are monosyllables).

The victims

Anthem for Doomed Youth takes a totally different approach to remembering the dead. Many of the fine young men have become the victims of war: all appear 'doomed'. (Owen originally called the poem *Anthem for DEAD Youth* – even more final, but without the sense of fate oppressing them.) The difference, of course, is that Owen completed the poem in 1917, after six months on the Western Front.

Metaphor

The poem is based on a series of metaphors on one central subject. The things associated with peacetime funerals are compared to their equivalents in the trenches. Try to list all these (e.g. church bells/guns) and see if you can find a change in the choice of material between the octave and the sestet.

The use of alliteration and onomatopoeia in *Anthem for*

For the Fallen (September 1914)

With proud thanksgiving, a mother for her children,
England mourns for her dead across the sea.
Flesh of her flesh they were, spirit of her spirit,
Fallen in the cause of the free.

Solemn the drums thrill: Death august and royal
Sings sorrow up into immortal spheres.
There is music in the midst of desolation
And a glory that shines upon our tears. ·

They went with songs to the battle, they were young,
Straight of limb, true of eye, steady and aglow.
They were staunch to the end against odds uncounted,
They fell with their faces to the foe.

They shall grow not old, as we that are left grow old.
Age shall not weary them, nor the years condemn.
. At the going down of the sun and in the morning
We will remember them.

They mingle not with their laughing comrades again;
They sit no more at familiar tables of home;
They have no lot in our labour of day-time;
They sleep beyond England's foam.

But where our desires are and our hopes profound,
Felt as a well-spring that is hidden from sight,
To the innermost heart of their own land they are known
As the stars are known to the Night;

As the stars that shall be bright when we are dust,
Moving in marches upon the heavenly plain,
As the stars that are starry in the time of our darkness,
To the end, to the end, they remain.

Laurence Binyon (1869–1943)

august: majestic
immortal spheres: reference to the classical idea of the music of the spheres

The main type of metaphor used in this poem is personification: giving non-personal things human qualities. What is personified in the first stanza? Can you find the same personification in another poem in this section?

Alliteration

Doomed Youth might be considered excessive: we have marked two lines in the text. See how many more examples you can find and try to work out why Owen over-uses these two techniques. There is evidence that he laboured through many drafts of this poem, with the assistance of Siegfried Sassoon, so these excessive sound-effects are certainly by choice, not carelessness. What do you think Owen's purpose was?

With Laurence Binyon's *For the Fallen*, we are back in the early days of war and the same rather naive patriotism as Rupert Brooke's. There are differences, however: the sense of sincerity in *The Soldier* is mostly absent here, not only because it is less personal, but because Binyon is drawn to unconvincing images and phrases that seem to belong to the ripping yarns of imperial heroism.

Heroism

'Steady and aglow' and 'staunch to the end against odds uncounted' are typical: you should be able to find many more. It is worth pointing out that in '*Solemn* the drums *thrill*', the two metaphors are nearly contradictory. It is early enough in the war for the idea of 'the cause of the free' to mean something and the ending (transporting the fallen to the stars) invites another comparison with Brooke.

Peace

What is astonishing is that this rather unconvincing poem contains a four-line stanza which is still one of the most moving reminders of the fallen even today. The fourth stanza is still heard regularly at Remembrance services: in its simple dignity and reminder of the eternal youth of the victims, now at peace, it retains its emotional power. Why is it so different from the rest of the poem?

Diction

Examine the differences in the vocabulary of stanza four and that of the other six stanzas. Perhaps Binyon found inspiration from Shakespeare:

'Age cannot wither her, nor custom stale
Her infinite variety.' *(Antony and Cleopatra)*

If so, he used it well.

Siegfried Sassoon's *Memorial Tablet* deals with the other great symbol of remembrance. If you need to be convinced of the horror of World War One, examine a war memorial. Compare the numbers of soldiers killed in World War One and World War Two (two years longer, and with a horrifying death toll of its own) or note how a small village can fill a memorial tablet with its dead. But Sassoon is not remembering the dead so much as satirising those who made them victims.

Sonnet

Memorial Tablet (Great War)

Squire nagged and bullied till I went to fight,
(Under Lord Derby's Scheme). I died in hell –
(They called it Passchendaele). My wound was slight,
And I was hobbling back; and then a shell
Burst slick upon the duck-boards: so I fell
Into the bottomless mud, and lost the light.

At sermon-time, when Squire is in his pew,
He gives my gilded name a thoughtful stare;
For, though low down upon the list, I'm there:
'*In proud and glorious memory*'... that's my due.
Two bleeding years I fought in France, for Squire:
I suffered anguish that he's never guessed.
Once I came home on leave: and then went west...
What greater glory could a man desire?

Siegfried Sassoon

Lord Derby: director of recruiting, 1915–16

Passchendaele: 3rd Battle of Ypres (Belgium), July–November 1917. Over 300,000 British casualties

Do you notice anything unusual about the form of this sonnet?

Drummer Hodge: A Comparison

Thomas Hardy (1840-1928) was still writing poetry during World War One and we shall look at his *In the Time of 'The Breaking of Nations'* elsewhere. But it is interesting to compare his *Drummer Hodge*, written during the Boer War some 15 years earlier, with *The Soldier* and *For the Fallen*. Drummer Hodge from Wessex is buried in the strange South African landscape: 'veldt', 'kopje' and so on.

Patriotism

Brooke and Binyon would have seen this as part of England. Hardy, more international in his sympathies, wrote:

'Yet portion of that unknown plain
    Will Hodge for ever be;
His homely Northern breast and brain
    Grow to some Southern tree,
And strange-eyed constellations reign
    His stars eternally.'

Satire

This is a bitter poem, notably in the *irony* of the last line: 'What greater glory could a man desire?' The use of a widely-used phrase about glory (to be taken with the opposite meaning) resembles Owen's *Dulce et Decorum est*. Compare the two and see if you can find other similarities; also contrast differences in tone or mood.

Memorial Tablet tells of a villager killed in war who in imagination (or as a ghost) sees the village squire (who forced him to join up) looking at his name on the tablet in church. The poem attacks the empty patriotism and prejudice of the ruling class. The class system is so powerful that the villager fought for the squire (who, of course, stayed at home), not for king and country. Even now the labourer's name is 'low down upon the list'. Who appears at the top of the list? If you can't guess, most war memorials will tell you. The heroism of Binyon's poem is long forgotten: death can be squalid and almost accidental, and it is not always possible to die 'with their faces to the foe'.

The enemy

And who is the foe? In Binyon's poem the Germans are the enemy, but who are the enemies of Sassoon and his farm-worker? Are the views of Sassoon and the character he created the same?

Diction

Much of the power of the poem comes from the *colloquial* language: the language of ordinary speech. The soldier breaks off into little asides, as in conversation; he uses slang; but best of all he uses words (often slang) with two meanings: 'went west' (died/went to the Western Front, perhaps); 'lost the light' (couldn't see/died). You can probably work out the two meanings of 'bleeding' for yourself.

The innocent heroism of the early poems seemed less and less appropriate in a war in which a typical soldiers' song contained the lines:

> 'If you want the old battalion,
> I know where they are –
> They're hanging on the old barbed wire.'

The optimistic heroism of the opening months had turned into mass slaughter.

■ The home front

The Send-Off

Down the close, darkening lanes they sang their way
To the siding-shed,
And lined the train with faces grimly gay.

Their breasts were stuck all white with wreath and spray
As men's are, dead.

Dull porters watched them, and a casual tramp
Stood staring hard,
Sorry to miss them from the upland camp.
Then, unmoved, signals nodded, and a lamp
Winked to the guard.

So, secretly, like wrongs hushed-up, they went.
They were not ours:
We never heard to which front these were sent.

Nor there if they yet mock what women meant
Who gave them flowers.

Shall they return to beatings of great bells
In wild train-loads?

A few, a few, too few for drums and yells,
May creep back, silent, to still village wells
Up half-known roads.

Wilfred Owen

siding-shed: shed on a railway siding: they do not use the main station
spray: small bunch of flowers

Metaphor

Look at the three phrases marked with this icon: two similes ('*as* men's are, dead' and '*like* wrongs hushed-up') and one metaphor ('*winked* to the guard'). In two cases the surface point of comparison is obvious: flowers are a feature of both celebrations and funerals, and the lamp flashed briefly like someone winking. But all three have something important to say about the attitudes of civilians and the fate of the soldiers. Try to work out why these comparisons are so effective.

The attitude of soldiers to civilians suggests that the feelings of 'we're all in this together' that applied in World War Two were conspicuously absent in World War One. The soldier-poets characterised the Home Front as given over to selfishness, opportunism and a dangerous and ignorant patriotism. This was a war in which the young men who did not sign up for the forces were sent white feathers for cowardice.

Patriotism

Several of Owen's poems deal with 'armchair patriots', including *S.I.W.* and *Dulce et Decorum Est*. In *S.I.W.*, 'Father would sooner him dead than in disgrace', but when the boy dies, it is by a self-inflicted wound – suicide – after his courage has 'leaked' away from months at the front. The parents are consoled with the news that 'Tim died smiling'.

The victims

Famously, *Dulce et Decorum Est* ends with an attack on 'my friend' who tells the 'old Lie' that it is good to die for your country. The poem was originally to be called *To Jessie Pope*, a well-known patriotic writer.

In this section we consider another poem by Owen, plus two poems with a startling hatred for elements of civilian society.

The Send-Off is one of Owen's finest poems, a masterpiece of restrained anger. The story is simple enough: a regiment goes to war, with little attention from the locals, and Owen poses questions about how many will return. Every detail in the poem contributes to the impression that they belong in a different world from the civilians, who have no interest in them.

Diction

For instance, look at the diction of lines 6–10. Every adjective tells of lack of interest, and Owen even involves things and objects: you will find them metaphorically as little involved as the people. It's a conspiracy of silence. Then there are mysterious phrases that bear more than one meaning. What does 'They were not ours' mean in line 12? Why are the roads 'half-known' in line 20? Lines 14–15 obviously mean that some might have survived despite the funeral-type flowers, but do they also mean that the women *meant* to send the soldiers to their deaths?

The enemy

In line 3 there is a wonderful two-word summary of false optimism. 'Grimly gay' is an example of an *oxymoron*: an instant contradiction, like 'bitter-sweet'. How could the men be grim and yet gaily happy?

Fight to a Finish

The boys came back. Bands played and flags were flying,
    And Yellow-Pressmen thronged the sunlit street
To cheer the soldiers who'd refrained from dying,
    And hear the music of returning feet.
'Of all the thrills and ardours War has brought,
This moment is the finest.' (So they thought.)

Snapping their bayonets on to charge the mob,
    Grim Fusiliers broke ranks with glint of steel,
At last the boys had found a cushy job.

*

    I heard the Yellow-Pressmen grunt and squeal;
And with my trusty bombers turned and went
To clear those Junkers out of Parliament.

Siegfried Sassoon

Yellow-Pressmen: The Yellow Press was what we might call the 'gutter press',
particularly chauvinistic newspapers
cushy: the common First World War slang word for 'easy'
Junkers: young German nobles, particularly of the military class

Judas and the Profiteer

Judas descended to this lower Hell
    To meet his only friend – the profiteer –
Who, looking fat and rubicund and well,
    Regarded him, and then said with a sneer,
'Iscariot, they did you! Fool! to sell
For silver pence the body of God's Son,
Whereas from maiming men with tank and shell
    I gain at least a golden million.'
But Judas answered: 'You deserve your gold;
It's not His body but His soul *you've* sold!"

Osbert Sitwell (1892–1969)

Judas Iscariot: betrayed Christ for 30 pieces of silver
profiteer: one who exploits war for profit, including arms sales
rubicund: red-faced

The poems by Sassoon and Sitwell are remarkable in their savagery. It is worth noting who the writers were: both were army officers (Sitwell was a regular), both from aristocratic families (Sir Osbert Sitwell was a baronet) and both became highly respected literary figures, yet both are violent in their condemnation of elements of society.

The enemy

Who was the enemy? Neither would have answered: 'The Germans', although it was the Germans they fought against. For Sassoon, it was the *chauvinists*. Recently this word has gained a new meaning ('male chauvinists', etc.) but chauvinism is really about extreme and war-like patriotism.

Diction

The first six lines of *Fight to a Finish* seem normal enough. However, it is interesting to see which words you would expect to find in a poem about troops returning from war, and which deliberately don't fit. What about the use of 'refrained from dying', and what do you make of 'the thrills and ardours' of war? Then, in line 7, Sassoon's hatred explodes: no longer is he the satirist in control. 'At last the boys had found a cushy job' is chillingly matter-of-fact about his fantasy of slaughtering the Yellow Press. Nor do M.P.s escape, killed by '*trusty* bombers' (i.e. fusiliers). What does Sassoon imply by the use of 'trusty'? What effect do words like 'mob', 'grunt' and 'squeal' have when applied to the press or 'Junkers' when applied to M.P.s?

Satire

Judas and the Profiteer chooses a softer target (even Jessie Pope condemned profiteers), but Sitwell's attack is even more damning than Sassoon's. Sitwell's satire uses the most famous traitor of all. Judas has only one friend on earth, the profiteer, who thinks that Judas was under-paid for his great treachery. The details reveal the depth of Sitwell's moral outrage. Examine the first line again and work out just what Sitwell is saying about the state of the world. Work out exactly why Judas (a damned soul, of course) thinks that the profiteer deserves his gold.

Metaphor

In *The Parable of the Old Man and the Young*, Wilfred Owen also uses events in the Bible as a metaphor for the evil of the times. The modern version of Abraham is too proud to spare his son Isaac, and the poem ends:

'But the old man would not so, but slew his son,
And half the seed of Europe, one by one.'

Peace

Everyone Sang

Everyone suddenly burst out singing;
And I was filled with such delight
As prisoned birds must find in freedom,
Winging wildly across the white
Orchards and dark green fields; on – on – and out of sight.

Everyone's voice was suddenly lifted;
And beauty came like the setting sun:
My heart was shaken with tears; and horror
Drifted away... O, but Everyone
Was a bird; and the song was wordless; the singing will
    never be done.

Siegfried Sassoon

done: finished, over

What sort of effect does the repeated 'w' sound make on
the reader?

Returning, We Hear the Larks

Sombre the night is.
And, though we have our lives, we know
What sinister threat lurks there.

Dragging these anguished limbs, we only know
This poison-blasted track opens on our camp –
On a little safe sleep.

But hark! joy – joy – strange joy.
Lo! Heights of night ringing with unseen larks.
Music showering our upturned list'ning faces.

Death could drop from the dark
As easily as song –
But song only dropped,
Like a blind man's dreams on the sand
By dangerous tides,
Like a girl's dark hair for she dreams no ruin lies there,
Or her kisses where a serpent hides.

Isaac Rosenberg

Look at the choice of words: 'Hark', 'Lo', 'strange' and 'joy'. What do they
remind you of?

Peace

Peace obviously means the absence of war. However, in this section, we shall look at five poems, only one of which is about the end of the war. One captures a moment of peace on a battlefield, two emphasise the continuation of the ordinary, peaceful things of life, and one revisits a battlefield after the war has moved on.

Everyone Sang and *Returning, We Hear the Larks* give excellent scope for comparison. Both are about song and birds, and in each case the meaning hinges on comparisons about bird-song.

Everyone Sang is about the end of the war. For once, Sassoon writes of his

Metaphor

own feelings with uncomplicated joy: the anger and the message, even the Yellow Press, are briefly forgotten. The mood is of exhilaration and this is expressed in the metaphor, 'Everyone was a bird'. This appears in the last two lines, although you will be able to find earlier hints of it. Notice that 'Everyone' has a capital letter: what effect does this have? Can you find any hint of feelings other than joy?

Returning, We Hear the Larks captures a moment of joy and peace. In the first six lines, all is pain and gloom. Examine the diction of those lines and see how many words (in sound as well as meaning) suggest fear or agony.

The soldiers 'dragging these anguished limbs' might remind you of the

Diction

opening of Owen's *Dulce et Decorum Est*. Like that poem, sudden exclamations and repeated words break into the desperate return march: then it was gas, here it is joy! It could have been death, but this time it's the joy of lark-song. Notice that both Sassoon and Rosenberg use the repetition of a single, simple word to express a feeling of release: 'on – on – and out of sight'/'joy – joy – strange joy'.

Metaphor

Let us look at the key similes of the last four lines. Dreaming occurs twice: the blind man on the sand, the girl's dark hair. The blind man feels joy on the sand by dangerous tides, the girl feels joy despite the hidden serpent (like Eve, who succumbs to the wiles of the serpent). In these comparisons, what is Rosenberg saying about the joy he and the other soldiers now feel?

This poem is very much in the minority among First World War poems in using *free verse*: there is no regular rhyme or stanza pattern.

As the Team's Head-Brass

As the team's head-brass flashed out on the turn
The lovers disappeared into the wood.
I sat among the boughs of the fallen elm
That strewed the angle of the fallow, and
Watched the plough narrowing a yellow square
Of charlock. Every time the horses turned
Instead of treading me down, the ploughman leaned
Upon the handles to say or ask a word,
About the weather, next about the war.
Scraping the share he faced towards the wood,
And screwed along the furrow till the brass flashed
Once more.

The blizzard felled the elm whose crest
I sat in, by a woodpecker's round hole,
The ploughman said, 'When will they take it away?'
'When the war's over.' So the talk began –
One minute and an interval of ten,
A minute more and the same interval.
'Have you been out?' 'No.' 'And don't want to, perhaps?'
'If I could only come back again, I should.
I could spare an arm, I shouldn't want to lose
A leg. If I should lose my head, why, so,
I should want nothing more.... Have many gone
From here?' 'Yes.' 'Many lost?' 'Yes, a good few.
Only two teams work on the farm this year.
One of my mates is dead. The second day
In France they killed him. It was back in March,
The very night of the blizzard, too. Now if
He had stayed here we should have moved the tree.'
'And I should not have sat here. Everything
Would have been different. For it would have been
Another world.' 'Ay, and a better, though
If we could see all, all might seem good.' Then
The lovers came out of the wood again:
The horses started and for the last time
I watched the clods crumble and topple over
After the ploughshare and the stumbling team.

Edward Thomas

the fallow: patch of ground left with nothing growing
charlock: field mustard, a weed
Have you been out?: out to the Front, active service

Patriotism

As the Team's Head-Brass finds peace on a farm in (probably) Herefordshire. You will note Edward Thomas's love of his country in this poem: not in any way aggressive or heroic, but patriotism nonetheless. A narrative and conversation piece, it is written in leisurely *blank verse*. This means that, although there is no rhyme, each line contains a regular five stressed syllables. You may have met this in Shakespeare's plays and, like Shakespeare, Edward Thomas is not very strict in its use. The poem, while fairly long, is not difficult to understand, but take care before you start to distinguish who is speaking. Decide who speaks first in each burst of conversation, as they always alternate.

Peace

The story is set against a peaceful scene: a field, a ploughman with his team of horses pulling the plough, a wood, two unnamed lovers. The poet is, perhaps, in uniform, but has yet to go overseas. He and the ploughman talk about the war, life on the farm, etc. There is an absence of tension and drama, but not of significant meaning.

Diction

A few lines have been marked with the *diction* icon, as particularly good examples, but in fact, most of the poem makes the same effect. Look at the choice of words, the use of dialogue (sometimes a speech as simple as 'yes' or 'no'), the way in which lines end in mid-sentence with some quite homely word like 'then'. What feeling and impression does Edward Thomas create through the diction and, indeed, the verse?

Is the poem about how the war has changed everything or nothing? Find as much evidence as you can for change. There are many examples, but the most striking is the connection between the blizzard and the ploughman's mate. The destruction of the tree *symbolises* (stands for) his death in war. But there is also a practical connection: blizzard – tree down – death of worker – tree not removed.

What evidence is there that war changes nothing? In one sense, no evidence at all, because there have been changes, but perhaps it cannot change the things that really matter. Read the last four lines and see if you agree.

You should keep those last four lines in mind as you move on to read the next poem, by Thomas Hardy.

In Time of 'The Breaking of Nations'

Only a man harrowing clods
  In a slow silent walk
With an old horse that stumbles and nods
  Half asleep as they stalk.

Only thin smoke without flame
  From the heaps of couch-grass;
Yet this will go onward the same
  Though Dynasties pass.

Yonder a maid and her wight
  Come whispering by:
War's annals will fade into night
  Ere their story die.

Thomas Hardy (1840–1928)

'The Breaking of Nations': a quotation from the Book of Jeremiah in the Bible
couch-grass: weeds
Dynasties: royal houses, lines of rulers
wight: man (an old-fashioned 'country' choice of word)

Beaucourt Revisited

(Extracts: stanzas 1, 3, 6 and 7 of a seven-stanza poem)

I wandered up to Beaucourt: I took the river track,
And saw the lines we lived in before the Boche went back;
But Peace was now in Pottage, the front was far ahead,
The front had journeyed Eastward, and only left the dead.

The new troops follow after, and tread the ground we won,
To them 'tis so much hillside re-wrested from the Hun;
We only walk with reverence this sullen mile of mud;
The shell-holes hold our history, and half of them our blood.

I crossed the blood-red ribbon, that once was No Man's Land,
I saw a misty daybreak and a creeping minute-hand;
And here the lads went over, and there was Harmsworth shot,
And here was William lying – but the new men know them not.

And I said, 'There is still the river, and still the stiff stark trees:
To treasure here our story, but there are only these';
But under the white wood crosses the dead men answer low,
'The new men know not Beaucourt, but we are here – we know.'

A.P. Herbert (1890–1971)

Boche, Hun: soldiers' slang for the Germans

In Time of 'The Breaking of Nations' is a poem that demonstrates the magic of simplicity: using the most restrained of language, in the quietest of tones, it takes as its subject much of what is most important in life. Incidentally, the poem is supposedly inspired by an earlier war in another country, but Hardy dated it '1915' for publication, and it must be seen partly as a response to the Great War.

The first word of the poem is 'only'; the same word is repeated at the

beginning of the second stanza. These are the little things of life: slow labour, half-asleep livestock, smoke without flame. The word that turns the poem round is 'yet', exactly halfway through: these little things are in fact the essential things, especially when the shy lovers are added in the third stanza.

Diction   Notice what happens to the words and worlds of official power. 'Dynasties' is a most impressive word and 'annals' sounds formal and official, but they 'pass' and 'fade', destroyed by very modest little words. Humanity depends on work, crops, love, etc. – not on empires and kingdoms.

Now think about the *sound* of the poem. An example of alliteration (spread across three lines) has been marked. See if you can find another example and decide what effect the chosen sounds make. Then read the poem aloud and sense the rhythm of it: why is the third line so long?

Alliteration   *Beaucourt Revisited*, while not one of the best of war poems, is interesting in many ways. Its author, Sir Alan Herbert, was a highly successful writer of light verse, revues and musicals. Here, however, he shares many of the viewpoints of more intense poets, although his verse does tend to jog along.

The subject is unusual: revisiting a scene of intense fighting, now peacefully

behind the lines as the Allies' advance finally begins. Most interesting, though, is the theme common to veterans of the Western Front: that there is a secret only they and their comrades know. Those back home are separate and unknowing; here even the new troops seem alien to the

Peace   ground. The poem (including the stanzas not printed here) is full of names of soldiers and places. Don't worry that you don't know who or where they are; they are part of the secret.

Re-read stanza 6, the third printed. Do you find it a successful re-creation of battle? What exactly does 'a misty daybreak and a creeping minute-hand' mean?

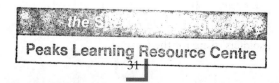

■ The higher ranks

The General

'Good morning; good morning!' the General said
When we met him last week on our way to the line.
Now the soldiers he smiled at are most of 'em dead,
And we're cursing his staff for incompetent swine.
'He's a cheery old card,' grunted Harry to Jack
As they slogged up to Arras with rifle and pack.

But he did for them both by his plan of attack.

Siegfried Sassoon

Arras: town in northern France, scene of battle in 1917

Diction

Although not so obvious as in Owen's *Inspection*, the diction in this poem is colloquial, suggesting soldiers' slang. See how many examples you can find. What do you think a 'cheery old card' is?

Base Details

If I were fierce, and bald, and short of breath,
    I'd live with scarlet Majors at the Base,
And speed glum heroes up the line to death.
    You'd see me with my puffy petulant face,
Guzzling and gulping in the best hotel, 🎵
    Reading the Roll of Honour. 'Poor
young chap',
I'd say – 'I used to know his father well;
    Yes, we've lost heavily in this last scrap.'
And when the war is done and youth stone dead,
I'd toddle safely home and die – in bed.

Siegfried Sassoon

Base Details: troops detailed for the base behind the lines
Roll of honour : list of the dead

Alliteration

'Guzzling and gulping' is both alliteration and onomatopoeia, but whatever you call it, it conveys a vivid impression of grossness and greed.
    The last line (or two lines) of each of these poems adds a punch to the satire. Think about how it works, then compare these to the poem on page 34, where Owen attempts to use Sassoon's style.

'Lions led by donkeys' is a phrase often quoted about the British troops in World War One. Today the image of the incompetent general sending troops over the top to certain death still survives: in the 1990s *Blackadder* provided the latest fictional version of it. Meanwhile, historians debate whether Field Marshal Haig, the overall British commander on the Western Front, was incompetent and fanatical, or a modern technical general. One thing is certain: it is virtually impossible to find any Great War poetry that praises the senior officers. They are either ignored in poetry, or presented as figures of fun or as the enemy, and frequently as both.

The enemy

Perhaps it would be more accurate to think of 'staff officers' rather than 'senior officers'. 'Line officers', actively involved in the front line, were rarely criticised by the soldier-poets, who were often line officers themselves. 'Staff officers', back at base, safely giving orders or despatching men and supplies to the front, were the target.

Satire

Satire can often be very comic and *The General* starts in a very jolly way, with the general cheerfully greeting the troops. This mood soon disappears in a poem that wastes no time in making its point: two lines meeting the general, two lines telling us of a horrific death-toll caused by incompetence, two lines contrasting the 'cheery old card' with the foot-sloggers and then, after the pause, the final punch.

Did you notice where the soldiers and the general met? 'On our way to the line' is a sort of No Man's Land where staff and troops might meet: the line and the base are different worlds, as the second poem shows. Notice also how the general finally becomes an active cause of death, almost a murderer.

Base Details begins in splendid style with a slanderous caricature of majors at the base: in both these poems Sassoon begins with a burst of energy and finishes with a downbeat, casually vicious throwaway line.

Diction

The vocabulary Sassoon uses about the majors is at the heart of his anger and his satire. List the words he uses to describe them and their actions and see what pattern of meaning emerges.

What does Sassoon want us to think about the phrase 'glum heroes'? Surely, if they were heroes, they would be glad to go up the line again? And why does he make the major refer to the soldier's father? What does this tell us about the major?

Inspection makes a different point from the Sassoon poems, although there is an overlap of meaning.

Inspection

'You! What d'you mean by this?' I rapped.
'You dare come on parade like this?'
'Please, sir, it's —' ' 'Old yer mouth,' the sergeant snapped.
'I takes 'is name, sir?' – 'Please, and then dismiss.'

Some days 'confined to camp' he got,
For being 'dirty on parade'.
He told me, afterwards, the damned spot
Was blood, his own. 'Well, blood is dirt,' I said.

'Blood's dirt,' he laughed, looking away
Far off to where his wound had bled
And almost merged for ever into clay.
'The world is washing out its stains,' he said.
'It doesn't like our cheeks so red:
Young blood's its great objection.
But when we're duly white-washed, being dead,
The race will bear Field-Marshal God's inspection.'

Wilfred Owen

damned spot: a quotation from *Macbeth*: Lady Macbeth, trying to wash away imaginary blood (and her guilt) says 'Out, damned spot!'

Before you read the page opposite, think of what is suggested by the word 'white'. It might be most easily done by considering what is the opposite of 'white'. You will find that some of the impact of this poem comes from putting two conflicting images of 'white' side by side.

Diction

'Something in Sassoon's style': Owen's *The Dead Beat*

In this poem, Wilfred Owen deliberately attempted to write a Sassoon-type satire. It's about a soldier who has broken down and is no longer fit for action. Is he genuine? Or is he malingering, 'putting on' his collapse? The target for Owen's attack on staff officers is the medical officer. The ending is very much in the style of Sassoon:

Satire

> 'Next day I heard the Doc.'s well-whiskied laugh:
> "That scum you sent last night soon died. Hooray."'

A bit exaggerated, surely – except that by those lines Owen wrote: 'Those are the very words!'

The enemy

The enemy is now more than the generals and staff officers, although they are part of it. The enemy is 'the world' – that is, the world of the older generation. This again sees a conspiracy of the old to wipe out the young, as in the *Parable of the Old Man and the Young,* referred to earlier. There is, incidentally, a hint of this in the last two lines of *Base Details*: the old (politicians, generals, businessmen) have led an evil world to war; the young must be sacrificed.

Diction

As a poet, Owen put his feelings in images, not argument, and the key image to start from is 'white'. What ideas does 'white' bring to your mind? Two possibilities, out of many, are white-as-clean (opposite: dirty) and white-as-pale/dead (opposite: red/blood). These two are deliberately and powerfully confused here. The establishment (the old/the officer class) punish dirt, but really their target is red-blooded youth. Eventually, everyone will be immaculately white (dead) and ready for God's inspection.

Inspection, from line 8 onwards, is a powerful poem; as a narrative and conversation piece it is perhaps less convincing. The role of Lieutenant Owen himself is interesting: he raps his question at the unfortunate soldier at the beginning, but is willing to listen to him later. It's almost as though there are two Owens here: at first he represents the system, then he becomes more personal, more sensitive. Certainly his glib retort, 'Well, blood is dirt', does him no credit.

The victims

The soldier/philosopher, severely wounded 'far off' on the front line, is a contrast to the parade ground exchanges: is this convincing or not?

Sassoon's anger and Owen's sensitivity might have caused them to make more of the dangerous incompetence of staff officers than most would, but the same failings (often dealt with in robust comedy) show up elsewhere. The 'incompetent swine' of *The General* are the same as the staff officers 'playing leapfrog' in the soldiers' song. As for cleanliness, A.P. Herbert wrote a gloriously offensive (and untitled) poem on the subject. The first stanza at least is repeatable:

> The General inspecting the trenches
> Exclaimed with a horrified shout,
> 'I refuse to command a Division
> Which leaves its excreta about'.

■ The Germans

Sonnet

To Germany

You are blind like us. Your hurt no man designed,
And no man claimed the conquest of your land.
But gropers both through fields of thought confined
We stumble and we do not understand.
You only saw your future bigly planned,
And we, the tapering paths of our own mind,
And in each other's dearest ways we stand,
And hiss and hate. And the blind fight the blind.

When it is peace, then we may view again
With new-won eyes each other's truer form
And wonder. Grown more loving-kind and warm
We'll grasp firm hands and laugh at the old pain,
When it is peace. But until peace, the storm
The darkness and the thunder and the rain.

Charles Sorley

A Dead Boche

To you who'd read my songs of War
And only hear of blood and fame,
I'll say (you've heard it said before)
'War's Hell!' and if you doubt the same,
Today I found in Mametz Wood
A certain cure for lust of blood:

Where, propped against a shattered trunk,
In a great mess of things unclean,
Sat a dead Boche; he scowled and stunk
With clothes and face a sodden green,
Big-bellied, spectacled, crop-haired,
Dribbling black blood from nose and beard.

Robert Graves (1895–1985)

who'd read: this is short for 'who would read' (i.e. who want to read) not 'who had read'
Mametz Wood: part of the front line on the Somme. The poem is dated '13 July, 1915'
Graves wished to suggest different feelings to the reader by his three uses of 'blood': can you work out what they are?

The enemy

Hatred for the Germans was surprisingly rare among the soldier-poets and, indeed, among the soldiers. When the Second World War broke out, people in Britain rightly felt that they had to oppose the evil of Nazism. There was nothing like that in 1914: the war was seen as a response to the Kaiser's imperial ambitions. It was being fought out between kingdoms and empires, the rulers of which were mostly cousins! No wonder Tommy and Fritz were seen as fellow-sufferers.

The victims

To Germany and *A Dead Boche* were both written within the first year of war. The octave of Sorley's sonnet gives a brief explanation of how war broke out. German ambition ('your future bigly planned') bumped into the 'tapering paths' of British security. Britain had no wish to attack ('Your hurt no man designed') but was determined to stand in the way of German aggression. But it was not the fault of the German people. They, like the British, were blind, led into conflict. The octave contains the word 'blind' three times: find three other words and phrases that suggest the same meaning.

Peace

The sestet deals almost exclusively with peace: the storm of war makes a brief reappearance at the end. What Sorley is looking forward to is peace between the peoples, not conquering the enemy. Look for indications of his belief that peace will mean seeing the Germans as they really are.

A Dead Boche has many interesting features, not least the fact that Robert Graves uses soldier-slang for German. He was half-German himself: Robert von Ranke Graves. His final description of the German inspires little personal sympathy: the soldier is not presented at all sentimentally, but as a rather unpleasant stereotype. Why, then, is the sight of him a cure for blood lust? Note, by the way, the opening two lines, which again cool the furious patriotism of the Home Front.

Try to make your own comparisons between these poems. Written by two young men of the same age and rank at the same time, neither of them feels any sympathy with the attitudes of warmongers, or any enmity for the German soldiers.

Patriotism

Are the poets unpatriotic? What, if anything, do they intend to do about their dislike for the war? How far do the poets share a viewpoint? What differences (in subject-matter, diction, etc.) are there in their ways of expressing their views?

This is No Case of Petty Right or Wrong

This is no case of petty right or wrong
That politicians or philosophers
Can judge. I hate not Germans, nor grow hot
With love of Englishmen, to please newspapers.
Beside my hate for one fat patriot
My hatred of the Kaiser is love true:-
A kind of god he is, banging a gong.
But I have not to choose between the two,
Or between justice and injustice. Dinned
With war and argument I read no more
Than in the storm smoking along the wind
Athwart the wood. Two witches' cauldrons roar.
From one the weather shall rise clear and gay;
Out of the other an England beautiful
And like her mother that died yesterday.
Little I know or care if, being dull,
I shall miss something that historians
Can rake out of the ashes when perchance
The phoenix broods serene above their ken.
But with the best and meanest Englishmen
I am one in crying, God save England, lest
We lose what never slaves and cattle blessed.
The ages made her that made us from dust:
She is all we know and live by, and we trust
She is good and must endure, loving her so:
And as we love ourselves we hate our foe.

Edward Thomas

Dinned: deafened
ken: knowledge
phoenix: a mythical bird that was destroyed by fire, but rose again from the ashes
perchance: perhaps

Diction

The diction in this poem undergoes great changes from the beginning, to the middle, to the end. The lines marked are typical. See if you can describe the different sorts of language.

Metaphor

The cauldron metaphor is difficult. Work out your own interpretation, then compare it with the one opposite.

This is No Case of Petty Right or Wrong is not an easy poem. It is worth persevering with, however, as it is the best summary of what many of the soldier-poets felt about the war in general, just as *Dulce et Decorum Est* is probably the best of many fine poems about being in action.

How can a patriot hate patriots? How can a man who feels no hatred for Germans regard them as hated foes? Difficult questions, but this poem answers them. Before examining the poem in detail, it is worth mentioning that it was written early in the war by a man of 36 or 37, too old to find the thought of war exciting.

Patriotism

To begin with, Thomas is in argumentative mood: he hates 'fat' patriots (i.e. those who sit at home and shout a lot), he has nothing against Germans, we are not necessarily in the right.

Be careful of the Kaiser-as-god metaphor: Thomas is not saying that the Kaiser is God. Note his use of a small 'g' for 'god' in line 7. Think what sort of gods you might associate with banging gongs, and then you will see the poet's picture of the Kaiser.

Complications start with the 'cauldrons' metaphor, when the mood

becomes more mystical. What was your interpretation of this? The cauldrons are the war, containing evil elements such as a witch's brew. Why two cauldrons? Britain and Germany? All is fire: 'smoking', 'roar', 'ashes'. As the fire dies, the clear day of peace and a restored England rise like a phoenix. Notice, though, that the England he knew is dead: 'her mother that died yesterday'.

Metaphor

Now we return to patriotism, but a different type from that of the fat patriots: purely a love of England. (Once again, a poet who sees his country as England, not Britain.) And for that re-creation of England, something more important than his feelings about Germans, patriots or politicians, he is forced to hate the enemy. Thomas does not hate Germans as Germans *per se*, but as a threat to the England he loves.

Patriotism

Did you notice that, as the poet becomes certain of his feelings in the last eight lines, he begins to write in rhyming couplets? Read this section again and decide what it is that makes him love England. 'We lose what never slaves and cattle blessed' is a key line.

Break of Day in the Trenches

The darkness crumbles away.
It is the same old druid Time as ever,
Only a live thing leaps my hand,
A queer sardonic rat,
As I pull the parapet's poppy
To stick behind my ear.
Droll rat, they would shoot you if they knew
Your cosmopolitan sympathies
(And God knows what antipathies).
Now you have touched this English hand
You will do the same to a German
Soon, no doubt, if it be your pleasure
To cross the sleeping green between.
It seems you inwardly grin as you pass
Strong eyes, fine limbs, haughty athletes,
Less chanced than you for life,
Bonds to the whims of murder,
Sprawled in the bowels of the earth,
The torn fields of France.
What do you see in our eyes
At the shrieking iron and flame
Hurled through still heavens?
What quaver – what heart aghast?
Poppies whose roots are in men's veins
Drop, and are ever dropping;
But mine in my ear is safe –
Just a little white with the dust.

Isaac Rosenberg

druid: priest of an ancient religion, suggesting the eternity of time
sardonic: mocking, scornful
droll: strange, comical
cosmopolitan: belonging to many different countries
sympathies/antipathies: feelings for and against

The Turkish Trench Dog (last eight lines)

Nearer and nearer like a wolf he crept –
That moment had my swift revolver leapt –
But terror seized me, terror born of shame
Brought flooding revelation. For he came
As one who offers comradeship deserved,
An open ally of the human race,
And sniffing at my prostrate form unnerved
He licked my face!

Geoffrey Dearmer 40

Break of Day in the Trenches is probably the best known poem by Isaac Rosenberg. Its distinctive tone is a gentle mockery covering serious themes. Rosenberg clearly shares the rat's 'cosmopolitan sympathies', and the ending evokes the temporary nature of life in the trenches in a movingly understated way.

This is partly done by the image of the poppy. When first mentioned in the poem, it is just a poppy; by the second mention it is a metaphor for men's blood. What does the poppy mean today? What did it mean to Rosenberg? He, after all, wore it almost like a badge.

Metaphor

You will find in this poem some fine description of the hellish landscape of the trenches: even the darkness 'crumbles away': a precise metaphor which suggests that the world revealed by dawn is falling apart. You will also find a powerful contrast between the 'haughty athletes' and the quavering of their hearts.

What the poem has to say about Britons and Germans is made the stronger by the choice of the rat as the alternative. We don't have a high opinion of rats, but this one is 'sardonic', as though mocking the soldiers. Why not? He has definite advantages over them. Examine the poem, finding all the signs of the rat's superiority.

Rosenberg himself brings a cynical humour to the poem at times: 'they would shoot you...' is neatly absurd, and he relishes the fact that it is the rat inwardly grinning as he passes fine young heroes. In fact the rat and the poppies (together with the other things we have considered) represent the new heroism: surviving.

Heroism

The Turkish Trench Dog is not actually about the Germans, but their Turkish allies. However, it shares the internationalism of Rosenberg's poem. Here, the Turkish dog takes the place of the rat. For over twenty lines Dearmer builds up the terror: he is near the Turkish lines at night when the dog approaches him with 'glowing eyes' and 'snuffling muzzle'. It will attack him, he will be discovered. The last line is an anti-climax of relief. It's an effect you have probably used yourself: stories ending 'then I woke up.'

But this poem has more to it than that. In particular, think about the line 'An open ally of the human race'. The dog can form an alliance between the canine and human worlds: all we can do is divide into Britain and her allies, or Germany and her allies.

Dulce et Decorum est

Bent double, like old beggars under sacks,
Knock-kneed, coughing like hags, we cursed through sludge,
Till on the haunting flares we turned our backs,
And towards our distant rest began to trudge.
Men marched asleep. Many had lost their boots
But limped on, blood-shod. All went lame; all blind;
Drunk with fatigue; deaf even to the hoots
Of tired, outstripped Five-Nines that dropped behind.

Gas! Gas! Quick, boys! – An ecstasy of fumbling,
Fitting the clumsy helmets just in time;
But someone still was yelling out and stumbling,
And flound'ring like a man in fire or lime...
Dim, through the misty panes and thick green light,
As under a green sea, I saw him drowning.
In all my dreams, before my helpless sight,
He plunges at me, guttering, choking, drowning.

If in some smothering dreams, you too could pace
Behind the wagon that we flung him in,
And watch the white eyes writhing in his face,
His hanging face, like a devil's sick of sin;
If you could hear, at every jolt, the blood
Come gargling from the froth-corrupted lungs,
Obscene as cancer, bitter as the cud
Of vile, incurable sores on innocent tongues, –
My friend, you would not tell with such high zest
To children ardent for some desperate glory,
The old Lie: *Dulce et decorum est*
Pro patria mori.

Wilfred Owen

Five-Nines: gas-shells. This line exists in various versions, the most common
alternative being 'Of gas-shells dropping softly behind'
misty panes: of the gas-helmet
guttering: melting, like a candle
Dulce et decorum est pro patria mori: a quotation from an ode by the Latin poet
Horace, meaning 'It is sweet and honourable to die for one's country'

Probably the best-known (and certainly one of the finest) battlefield poems in English, Wilfred Owen's *Dulce et Decorum est* is divided into three clearly separate sections. Each of them consists of an eight-line stanza (rhyming ABABCDCD), with an extra four lines at the end for the main message of the poem.

Metaphor

Throughout the poem the use of comparisons, both metaphor and simile, is highly pointed: they are not used solely to increase drama, but also to reveal layers of meaning. Perhaps, before you read on, you could look at the three similes marked opposite and try to work out why Owen used them.

Heroism

The first stanza is a fine summary of surviving against the odds. These men are returning from the flares of the battlefield to their 'distant rest', but they are no longer the young men who joined up. The metaphor 'cursed through sludge' suggests that only the violence of their language drives them forward; the metaphor 'blood-shod' echoes 'blood-shot', but tells us that their feet are covered in blood. ('Shod' is the same as 'shoed'; it is as though they are wearing blood, not boots.) Above all, they have become old people: you should be able to find at least four metaphors or similes in the first eight lines that compare them to the very aged. Even the unwounded are in a state of collapse.

Diction

In the second stanza, the tempo changes, from men too slow to react to the sudden explosion of 'Gas! Gas! Quick, boys!' Here, and in the third stanza, Owen uses diction and comparisons that bring feelings of sickness and revulsion to the reader: look at the double use of 'drowning' instead of a normal rhyme. What have you decided about the simile of fire and lime? Surely Owen means us to remember that these are two things used to destroy human remains: in cremation or in the use of quick-lime for the bodies of murderers, etc.

This is already a poem of enormous power, which impresses and disgusts the reader simultaneously, but the final section has still greater impact. The bad dreams of Owen, late in stanza two, begin the torment of the eye-witness and stanza three turns this round to confront the reader: 'If...*you* could pace'. Look at the diction, the metaphors and the similes in stanza three and you find an added dimension: now they are corrupt and evil. You will also find some dramatic and sickening verbs (especially present participles, the '-ing' form of the verb): find examples and assess their effect on the reader.

The Happy Warrior

His wild heart beats with painful sobs,
His strain'd hands clench at ice-cold rifle,
His aching jaws grip a hot parch'd tongue,
His wide eyes search unconsciously.

He cannot shriek.

Bloody saliva
Dribbles down his shapeless jacket.

I saw him stab
And stab again
A well-killed Boche.

This is the happy warrior,
This is he…

Herbert Read (1893–1968)

Julian Grenfell: The happy warrior?

There is one poem written by an officer at the Front which expresses no anger at war and much joy in life. *Into Battle* was written by Julian Grenfell (1888–1915) in April 1915 and is too long to print in full here, but lines 5–8 are typical:

> And life is colour and warmth and light,
>   And a striving evermore for these;
> And he is dead who will not fight;
>   And who dies fighting has increase.

But Julian Grenfell was unique. A regular army officer, celebrated sportsman and son of the formidable Lady Desborough, he was an odd mixture of rebel and admired establishment figure. He was shot and fatally wounded two weeks after writing the poem, partly because of his own careless heroism. A well-known writer of the day (a former schoolfriend of Grenfell's) remarked that he was the only person who could have written *Into Battle* and meant it sincerely.

Patriotism

The fascinating point about the third stanza is that, by what should be the end of it (line 8), Owen still has not reached the main clause of the only sentence in this stanza: it is still at the stage of 'If you…'. The result? We can hardly wait for his main point and, when it comes, it brings another twist. 'My friend' narrows the reader down to one person, the armchair patriot typified by Jessie Pope (see **The Home Front** section).

You can find more vivid, violent and disturbing description in this poem (it is a descriptive masterpiece), but you should also see how cleverly Owen shifts his viewpoint throughout the poem: at one time we feel ourselves being targeted and sharing the horror and the bad dreams, before Owen finally strikes against the enemy on the Home Front.

The Happy Warrior by Sir Herbert Read is a warning against any feeling we might have that Wilfred Owen over-dramatises, or feels the pity of war too acutely. Compared with Read, Owen is almost moderate. In *The Happy Warrior* no harm comes to the British soldier: he does what he is supposed to do, kill a German. Read even reminds us of a famous nineteenth-century poem, written by William Wordsworth in 1807:

> 'Who is the Happy Warrior? Who is he
> That every man in arms should wish to be?'

Note the sense of security in the comfortable rhyming couplet. Then turn to Read's version. The quotation from Wordsworth dissolves into choking silence in the last line; the soldier is almost an animal, a mad dog perhaps; the victor is described as a victim.

The victims

Poems dealing with the authentic excitement of battle are difficult to find, although some at the start of the war imagine the glory of fighting in a just war. The Grenfell poem opposite is almost unique among poems written at the Front in its love of life and free use of terms like 'noble' and 'courageous'. Why not investigate anthologies of war poetry and see if you can find others? You may well find *The Song of the Happy Warrior* by Rifleman Donald S. Cox, but, like the Read poem, it does not live up to its title.

The wounded and the dead

Futility

Move him into the sun –
Gently its touch awoke him once,
At home, whispering of fields unsown.
Always it woke him, even in France,
Until this morning and this snow.
If anything might rouse him now
The kind old sun will know.

Think how it wakes the seeds –
Woke, once, the clays of a cold star.
Are limbs so dear-achieved, are sides
Full nerved, – still warm, – too hard to stir?
Was it for this the clay grew tall?
O what made fatuous sunbeams toil
To break earth's sleep at all?

Wilfred Owen

unsown: or 'half-sown', depending on the edition. The overall meaning is unchanged
fatuous: here meaning 'pointless' (or 'futile')

Sonnet

A Charles Sorley sonnet is printed below, but is *Futility* also a sonnet?

Sonnet

When you see millions of the mouthless dead
Across your dreams in pale battalions go,
Say not soft things, as other men have said,
That you'll remember. For you need not so.
Give them not praise. For, deaf, how should they know
It is not curses heaped on each gashed head?
Nor tears. Their blind eyes see not your tears flow.
Nor honour. It is easy to be dead.
Say only this, 'They are dead'. Then add thereto,
'Yet many a better one has died before'.
Then, scanning all the o'ercrowded mass, should you
Perceive one face that you loved heretofore,
It is a spook. None wears the face you knew.
Great death has made all his for evermore.

Charles Sorley

46

Poems about the wounded and the dead are, of course, very common, but sometimes take an unexpected viewpoint. *Futility*, of course, is asking 'what's the point?' but extends this in the second stanza beyond 'what was the point of this young man growing up to die like this in the snow?' What is the question that Owen is asking in the last two lines?

Peace

Owen uses the English countryside as a peaceful contrast to war (as does Edward Thomas): the sun used to wake the dead man to his farm work. You might like to ask yourself how the soldier died. Are the Germans the only killers on the Western Front?

Sonnet

Futility also needs to be considered from the point of view of verse and form. Is it a sonnet? There could be long arguments over this, but, on balance, it probably is not. The uneven length of lines and the odd seven/seven division are untypical of sonnets, though it is a 14-line poem with a regular rhyme scheme. You may have found the rhyme scheme difficult to detect, because Owen employs *half-rhyme*, which means exactly what it says: 'sun' and 'sown' half rhyme. (It is common, though not essential, to use the same consonant – 's' in this case – in the half-rhyming words.) So the rhyme in each stanza is ABABCCC. Work through the poem, finding the half-rhymes and also the single pair of full rhymes in each stanza.

Owen questions the point of existence on the evidence of one death; Sorley finds a similar futility in the death of millions. There is no point honouring and weeping over the dead, because death now possesses all. There are no faces of loved ones among the dead, only ghosts ('spooks'). You will no doubt recognise some of the poets referred to in lines 3 and 4, the ones who said 'soft things' about remembering the dead. The sentence 'It is easy to be dead' carries the reverse meaning as well – it is difficult to be alive.

Heroism

Once again we are invited to ask: 'what is true courage – reckless heroism or patient survival?'

These two poems are powerfully pessimistic, but you will note that in both cases the language is very simple. The second stanza of *Futility* is more complicated than the extreme simplicity of stanza one ('The kind old sun will know') and *Sonnet* has occasional strong words like 'gashed', but generally both poems gain their impact by restraint.

Diction

Exposure

Our brains ache, in the merciless iced east winds that knive us...
Wearied we keep awake because the night is silent...
Low, drooping flares confuse our memory of the salient...
Worried by silence, sentries whisper, curious, nervous,
    But nothing happens.

Watching, we hear the mad gusts tugging on the wire,
Like twitching agonies of men among its brambles.
Northward, incessantly, the flickering gunnery rumbles,
Far off, like a dull rumour of some other war.
    What are we doing here?

The poignant misery of dawn begins to grow...
We only know war lasts, rain soaks, and clouds sag stormy.
Dawn massing in the east her melancholy army
Attacks once more in ranks on shivering ranks
of gray,
    But nothing happens.

Sudden successive flights of bullets streak the silence.
Less deadly than the air that shudders black with snow,
With sidelong flowing flakes that flock, pause and renew;
We watch them wandering up and down the wind's nonchalance,
    But nothing happens.

Pale flakes with fingering stealth come feeling for our faces –
We cringe in holes, back on forgotten dreams, and stare, snow-dazed
Deep into grassier ditches. So we drowse, sun-dozed,
Littered with blossoms trickling where the blackbird fusses.
    Is it that we are dying?

Slowly our ghosts drag home: glimpsing the sunk fires, glozed
With crusted dark-red jewels; crickets jingle there;
For hours the innocent mice rejoice: the house is theirs;
Shutters and doors, all closed: on us the doors are closed, –
    We turn back to our dying.

Since we believe not otherwise can kind fires burn;
Nor ever suns smile true on child, or field, or fruit.
For God's invincible spring our love is made afraid;
Therefore, not loath, we lie out here; therefore were born,
    For love of God seems dying.

Exposure is more ambitious in style than *Futility*, but you will find it interesting to make comparisons between the two. In terms of style, compare the use of half-rhyme. In terms of theme, the main point of comparison is the identification of the weather as an enemy.

The enemy

In *Exposure*, one of the keys to Owen's meaning lies in those short final lines outside the rhyme scheme. Of eight stanzas, four end in 'But nothing happens' and three in some variant on 'Is it that we are dying?' The conclusion is obvious: they can be dying even when nothing happens. The weather itself is fatal.

Metaphor

On the opposite page, a metaphor ('Dawn massing... ranks of gray') is marked for you. How does this metaphor contribute to the idea of the weather-as-enemy? In the fourth stanza, you should notice the comparison of bullets and snow-black air, which adds to the same effect. The last stanza then puts together a frosty night and a burying party with eyes of ice.

Alliteration

The sense of exposure is frequently brought out by the sound of the poem: the first line, with the howling of the wind suggested by the near-rhyme of 'iced'/'east', sets the tone for the poem. Three examples of alliteration, onomatopoeia or both have been marked, but there are many more. Examine for yourself Owen's use of sound in this poem, taking these three examples as a starting-point. It should be remembered that effects can be obtained by rhythm as well as by repeated consonants: 'flakes that flock, pause and renew', with its comma pause at the word 'pause', creates the movement of the snow.

The second-last stanza is surprising. Owen's patriotism was not in doubt,

Patriotism

but his usual emphasis on the pity of war is somewhat undermined here by the phrase 'not loath', suggesting that he and his comrades were not unwilling to lie out there. However, this is explained by the fact that it is, he believes, the only way to restore peace in 'God's invincible spring'. The mood of the poem remains pessimistic. Look at the surrounding stanzas. Home no longer belongs to these ghosts of men: they seem to be dying; God's love seems to be dying. The poem then ends with the burying party and the frosts of night.

Tonight, His frost will fasten on this mud and us,
Shrivelling many hands, puckering foreheads crisp.
The burying-party, picks and shovels in their shaking grasp,
Pause over half-known faces. All their eyes are ice,
    But nothing happens.

Wilfred Owen

salient: angle in the front line
nonchalance: coolness, casualness – in this sense, the wind's casual changes of direction
glozed: normal meaning: 'flatter in words'. Owen probably means 'flattered' in the sense of 'showed to advantage'; possibly he was tempted by the sound of the word
loath: unwilling

The Dug-Out

Why do you lie with your legs ungainly huddled,
And one arm bent across your sullen, cold,
Exhausted face? It hurts my heart to watch you,
Deep shadow'd from the candle's guttering gold;
And you wonder why I shake you by the shoulder;
Drowsy, you mumble and sigh and turn your head...
You are too young to fall asleep for ever;
And when you sleep you remind me of the dead.

Siegfried Sassoon

Peace

This poem was written in France in July 1918, only four months before the end of the war, though much was still to happen. The Germans' last big offensive on the Marne was just starting, Sassoon had still to receive the head wound that ended his war and Wilfred Owen was still alive. This poem, however, vividly reflects the fact that Sassoon has spent four years at war. How?

By now, you should see that poems about the wounded and the dead are not always what you would expect. Death is not necessarily a sudden, dramatic thing. Sorley regards it as 'easy'. Owen finds the border to death blurred, the soldier in *Futility* sinks undetected into death, the poet in *Exposure* wonders if it has already started.

As for wounds, they may or may not be inflicted deliberately by the enemy. Owen's *S.I.W.*, for instance, deals with a self-inflicted wound. This poem, already referred to in **The Home Front** section, is long, ambitious and uneven in quality, and it presents the soldier as victim oppressed by a variety of enemies.

S.I.W. is in four sections. The first, the prologue, is much the longest. It presents a rather sentimental view of a poor suffering 'lad', whose 'courage leaked' through 'month after month' of being shelled without respite. He misses every chance of escape, including being wounded. Soldiers actually envied their colleagues a 'blighty' (a wound serious enough to send the victim back to Britain). 'The lad' falls victim to 'this world's powers', his family ('death sooner than dishonour' says his father) and his own code of honour (he thinks it 'vile' to shoot oneself in the hand, as some do).

The victims

Inevitably, his only way out is to commit suicide by shooting himself. The last of the four sections, after a rather laborious psychological analysis, is a brief epilogue:

> 'With him they buried the muzzle his teeth had kissed,
> And truthfully wrote the Mother, "Tim died smiling".'

A poem like this questions all our assumptions about patriotism and honour. Through no fault of his own, Tim is incapable of the greater heroism: surviving.

Though 'smiling' has an extra, bloody meaning, it and 'kissed' suggest that death is the soldier's friend. This is part of the secret no-one on the Home Front is allowed to share.

Heroism

The Dug-Out finds pain everywhere. How do you distinguish the dead from the barely alive?

This is a gentle poem: no attacks, no shells, relatively safe in the dug-out.

But the words used about the young soldier echo the words of more violent poems like *Dulce et Decorum est*. After four years of war, even sleep scares Sassoon. Compare the last lines of this poem with those of Charles Sorley's *Sonnet*. Do they basically mean the same thing?

Diction

■ Sleep and dreams of death

Lights Out

I have come to the borders of sleep,
The unfathomable deep
Forest where all must lose
Their way, however straight,
Or winding, soon or late;
They cannot choose.

Many a road and track
That, since the dawn's first crack,
Up to the forest brink,
Deceived the travellers,
Suddenly now blurs,
And in they sink.

Here love ends,
Despair, ambition ends;
All pleasure and all trouble,
Although most sweet or bitter,
Here ends in sleep that is sweeter
Than tasks most noble.

There is not any book
Or face of dearest look
That I would not turn from now
To go into the unknown
I must enter, and leave, alone,
I know not how.

The tall forest towers;
Its cloudy foliage lowers
Ahead, shelf above shelf;
Its silence I hear and obey
That I may lose my way
And myself.

Edward Thomas

that: (in second-last line): so that

The metaphor of sleep-as-a-forest is never far away in this poem. Try to trace the metaphor through the five stanzas.

Metaphor

Visions of death were an inevitable theme of First World War poetry. Wilfred Owen's flawed, but memorable, *Strange Meeting* was his last poem and its ending, in the broken line 'Let us sleep now...', led to the (incorrect) assumption that he was killed without completing it. *Lights Out*, a gentler and more controlled vision, is not technically a Great War poem, but, given its theme and time of composition, it is worthy of inclusion.

Metaphor

This poem is based on two metaphors. By now you should have examined the sleep/forest one for yourself. However, there is also a secret metaphor: all metaphors are implied comparisons, this is a concealed comparison. The poem pretends to be about sleep, yet the sensitive reader must feel that it is about death. 'Lights out' suggests camp routine and also the extinguishing of the light of life.

Diction

It is often in the simplest words (and the shortest lines) that Thomas creates a sense of finality:

'Here love ends,'
'That I may lose my way
And myself.'

Thomas was much older than the other soldier-poets and, although he died before the age of 40, there is less of the sense of waste, of hopes not fulfilled, in this than in other poems on the same theme. Instead, it is a remarkably serene piece.

Peace

He loses his way in the deep forest, but he is meant to do so. That is the way things are. Examine the poem and find evidence to prove that Thomas is happy to sink into 'the unfathomable deep/forest'.

Strange Meeting begins:

'It seemed that out of battle I escaped
Down some profound dull tunnel.'

Owen then realises that he is in hell, and meets a dead man whose words take up the rest of the poem. Owen transfers much of his own feeling to this man, the sense of 'the undone years', for instance. Eventually, he realises that the dead man is a German soldier he has killed. Owen worked through many drafts of this poem, but it still often reads awkwardly. However, it also contains two of the most memorable sentences of Great War poetry. Owen echoes his own preface in the lines:

'I mean the truth untold,
The pity of war, the pity war distilled.'

The enemy

'I am the enemy you killed, my friend' is the final unanswerable response to the question, 'Who is the enemy?'

An Irish Airman Foresees his Death

I know that I shall meet my fate
Somewhere among the clouds above;
Those that I fight I do not hate,
Those that I guard I do not love;
My country is Kiltartan Cross,
My countrymen Kiltartan's poor,
No likely end could bring them loss
Or leave them happier than before.
Nor law, nor duty bade me fight,
Nor public men, nor cheering crowds,
A lonely impulse of delight
Drove to this tumult in the clouds;
I balanced all, brought all to mind,
The years to come seemed waste of breath,
A waste of breath the years behind
In balance with this life, this death.

W.B. Yeats (1865–1939)

Kiltartan: the airman's home village in Ireland

Edward Thomas: A Final Word

Although he himself was to face the dangers of war service and die in action, Edward Thomas had great compassion for others. In 1915 he joined the Army, but did not see active service until early 1917. Thus, when he wrote *In Memoriam (Easter, 1915)* he was writing of the sufferings of others. It is a tiny poem of four lines that sums up, without drama, the pity of war:

> The flowers left thick at nightfall in the wood
> This Eastertide call into mind the men,
> Now far from home, who, with their sweethearts, should
> Have gathered them and will do never again.

Where else can you find the linked image of flowers/death/soldiers in poetry or elsewhere? Where else did Thomas emphasise the importance of young men and their sweethearts? Why is Easter so appropriate?

An Irish Airman Foresees his Death is unusual in many ways. Firstly, it was written by a man who was already acknowledged as a great poet and playwright: Owen even used lines by W.B. Yeats as epigraphs or mottoes for at least two of his poems. Secondly, Yeats was a key figure in the Irish Nationalist movement. Ireland was still part of the United Kingdom (though not for many more years). When Yeats wrote a poem entitled *Easter 1916*, it was not about the Great War, but about the Easter Rising against the British in Ireland.

Let us define some of the ideas which occur in this poem which we can find in other Great War poetry.

The enemy

Yeats again considers who the enemy is or, more precisely, who the enemy is not. His airman has no reason to hate the Germans. Which other poets felt the same way? He also has no reason to love the British, as Kiltartan will not be affected whatever happens. Does this make him unique in the poems you have read? Why, then, did he volunteer? Because of 'a lonely impulse of delight'. Who else would have understood, even shared, this impulse?

Heroism

Yeats makes his airman speak of life and death in the same breath, as part of the same thing. Which other poets treated death as nothing to be afraid of? Add to the examples you have found these two:

'And the worst friend and enemy is but Death.'

(Rupert Brooke, *Peace*)

'Out there, we've walked quite friendly up to Death.'

(Wilfred Owen, *The Next War*)

Together with this feeling about death is unease with the world of pre-1914. This was mostly evident among the younger poets, though Yeats (decidedly not young) shared it with 'A waste of breath the years behind'. This can partially account for Grenfell's joyous involvement in war: in *Into Battle*, he writes of finding a 'newer birth'. Brooke (like Grenfell, a privileged figure and hugely admired) could write in *Peace* about 'a world grown old and cold and weary'.

Yeats, however, did not see active service: he was, after all, nearly 50 at the outbreak of war. What different qualities, emotions and viewpoints have you found in the poets who served on the Western Front? Try to write down as precise a summary as you can.

MCMXIV

Those long uneven lines
Standing as patiently
As if they were stretched outside
The Oval or Villa Park,
The crowns of hats, the sun
On moustached archaic faces
Grinning as if it were all
An August Bank Holiday lark;

And the shut shops, the bleached
Established names on the sunblinds,
The farthings and sovereigns,
And dark-clothed children at play
Called after kings and queens,
The tin advertisements
For cocoa and twist, and the pubs
Wide open all day –

And the countryside not caring:
The place names all hazed over
With flowering grasses, and fields
Shadowing Domesday lines
Under wheat's restless silence;
The differently-dressed servants
With tiny rooms in huge houses,
The dust behind limousines;

Never such innocence,
Never before or since,
As changed itself to past
Without a word – the men
Leaving the gardens tidy,
The thousands of marriages,
Lasting a little while longer:
Never such innocence again.

Philip Larkin (1922–1985)

twist: tobacco
Domesday lines: marks, still in the fields, of their shape in the Middle Ages: the Domesday Book was the first census (1086)

The First World War has entered the national memory. Though the Second World War may feature more in films, writers have felt a need to re-remember the Great War like no other. Even the 1995 Booker Prize went to a book (*The Ghost Road*) about the First World War. When Jon Stallworthy wrote a poem attacking poems about Vietnam, it was Wilfred Owen he singled out as a poet who sent 'dispatches from the Front'. The poets themselves were well aware of the historic significance of what they went through. Many of the survivors wrote autobiographies or fictionalised memoirs.

Modern poets are often struck by the suddenness with which a stable society was destroyed. The current Poet Laureate, Ted Hughes (born 1930), has written several poems about the Great War. In *Six Young Men*, an old photograph prompts him to contrast their still-apparent youth and life in the picture with the fact that six months later they were all dead. They live in 'six celluloid smiles'.

Both the Hughes poem and *MCMXIV* look back to peace: the peace before

Peace

the war. Philip Larkin's poem is simply a list: you will not find a full-stop or a main verb anywhere. The reigns of Edward VII (1901–10) and George V (the first years from 1910 to 1914) are a period which seems now to have been particularly peaceful, though servants and artisans must have found it less attractive. Larkin enjoys nostalgic memories. The faces are said to be 'archaic' (out of date, of a different age). See how many more details touch our fascination with the past: you could start by thinking about the title.

Even though the poem is part of our tendency to be sentimental about the past, the last stanza is genuinely moving. 'Never such innocence again' sums up the state of people cheerfully entering a war which they thought would be over by Christmas ('leaving the gardens tidy' for next year), only to be plunged into a present hell and a future changed beyond recognition.

'Never such innocence': in 1914 Rupert Brooke was a much more worldly and mature person than Wilfred Owen, yet in his poems he represents to us the national innocence that was soon lost. But remember that Brooke did not share Larkin's regard for the world of 1914: he wanted to change 'a world grown old and cold and weary', but could not have foreseen the horror of that change.

Self-test questions

Who? What? Why? When? Where? How?

1 Who did Owen meet in the poem *Strange Meeting*?
2 What did the Turkish trench dog do at the end of the poem of the same name?
3 Why did the labourer join up in the poem *Memorial Tablet*?
4 When did Isaac Rosenberg see 'a queer sardonic rat'?
5 Where did Rupert Brooke expect to be buried?
6 How did the general in Sassoon's poem of that name 'do for' the soldiers?
7 Who will miss the soldiers in *The Send-Off*?
8 When did Edward Thomas write *In Memoriam*?
9 What did Owen state was dirt in the poem *Inspection*?
10 Who did Edward Thomas describe as 'a kind of god, banging a gong'?

Open quotes

Complete the following quotations and identify where they come from:

1 'My subject is War…'
2 'The old Lie:…'
3 'Now the soldiers he smiled at…'
4 'As I pull the parapet's poppy…'
5 'Age shall not weary them…'
6 'Those that I fight I do not hate…'
7 'O what made fatuous sunbeams toil…'
8 'Not a drum was heard, not a funeral note…'
9 'If I should die,…'
10 'The new men know not…'
11 'Great Death has made…'
12 'Grinning as if it were all…'
13 'Today I found in Mametz Wood…'
14 'And strange-eyed constellations reign…'
15 'What passing-bells…'
16 'I died in hell…'
17 'Its silence I hear and obey…'
18 'If I were fierce, and bald…'
19 'Beside my hate for one fat patriot…'
20 'Bloody saliva/Dribbles…'

Two of the above quotations do not relate to World War One. Can you identify them? All the quotations appear in this book. If there are any you don't know, try to find them before looking at the answers.

Friends and enemies

Comment on what you have learned about the following poets' opinions of the people named:

1 Sassoon's opinion of staff officers.
2 Edward Thomas's opinion of the Germans.
3 Owen's opinion of armchair patriots.
4 Binyon's opinion of the fallen.
5 Thomas's opinion of the ploughman and the lovers.

How do they do that?

Each of the following lines makes use of at least one of the following poetic techniques: metaphor, simile, alliteration, onomatopoeia, unusual diction. See if you can identify them:

1 'Only the stuttering rifles' rapid rattle' (Owen)
2 'They shall grow not old, as we that are left grow old' (Binyon)
3 'Knock-kneed, coughing like hags, we cursed through sludge' (Owen)
4 'You'd see me with my puffy petulant face' (Sassoon)
5 'To clear those Junkers out of Parliament' (Sassoon)
6 'With sidelong flowing flakes that flock, pause and renew' (Owen)
7 'The unfathomable deep/Forest where all must lose/Their way' (Thomas)
8 'Her sights and sounds; dreams happy as her day' (Brooke)
9 'Like a blind man's dreams on the sands/By dangerous tides' (Rosenberg)
10 'I takes 'is name, sir?' – 'Please, and then dismiss.' (Owen)

Do you remember...

1 The names of three sonnets?
2 Who Lord Derby was?
3 What a Five-Nine was?
4 What 'dulce et decorum est pro patria mori' means...
5. ... and who first wrote it?
6 The home-town of the Irish airman?
7 Two slang names for the Germans?
8 Who Jessie Pope was?
9 Which poet makes use of half-rhyme...
10 ... and a poem where he uses it?
11 What the Yellow Press was?
12 Who Tommy Atkins was...
13 ... and who wrote a poem about him?
14 The real meaning of 'chauvinist'?
15 Who Harry and Jack were?

Themes and poems

Inevitably with the similarity of subject-matter, the same themes and subjects occur in several poems and by several poets. Compare what each of the following poems says about the themes given:

1 The natural world (sun/rain/flowers/woods, etc): The Soldier; As the Team's Head-Brass; Returning, We Hear the Larks; Break of Day in the Trenches; In Memoriam (Easter 1915).
2 The ordinary soldier: The General; Inspection; The Send-Off.
3 Sleep: For the Fallen; Lights Out; Strange Meeting; The Dug-Out.
4 The future: The Send-Off; Fight to a Finish; In Time of 'The Breaking of Nations'; For the Fallen.
5 Motives for going to war: An Irish Airman Foresees his Death; This is no Case of Petty Right or Wrong; Memorial Tablet; Into Battle; The Soldier.

Further reading

Find out as many of the answers to the following questions as you can. This will require research at your school, college or local library. You may not be able to find all the books mentioned, but you could recommend them to the librarian.

1 In The Collected Poems of Wilfred Owen you will find Smile, Smile, Smile, written six weeks before his death. In this poem, Owen says much about the relationship between soldiers and civilians and about the 'secret' the soldiers possess. Can you summarise his opinions?

2   You may find the poem *Vergissmeinnicht*, by Keith Douglas, in several anthologies: it is certainly in *The Oxford Book of Twentieth Century English Verse*. Keith Douglas wrote, and was killed, during World War Two. Compare the attitude he takes to Germans with the First World War poets.

3   In Chapter 20 of Robert Graves's autobiography, *Goodbye to All That*, he describes the incident he used in the poem *A Dead Boche*. Find the piece of description that is almost identical to the poem.

4   The play *Journey's End*, by R.C. Sheriff, is a famous drama of World War One, written in 1928 by a man who had served a year on the Western Front. In it the heroic Captain Stanhope has his own defence against the leaking of courage described by Owen in *S.I.W.* What is it?

5   To understand Edward Thomas's love of England, it is helpful to read his non-war poems. Find the small Faber paperback, *Selected Poems of Edward Thomas*, read *The Manor Farm* and decide what Manor Farm represents to the poet.

Self-test answers

Who? What? Why? When? Where? How?

1   The German he killed.
2   Licked the poet's (Dearmer's) face.
3   He was bullied by the local squire.
4   At dawn (break of day).
5   Some corner of a foreign field.
6   With his plan of attack.
7   The tramp.
8   Easter 1915.
9   Blood.
10 The Kaiser.

Open quotes

1   'My subject is War, and the pity of War.' (Owen: Preface)
2   'The old Lie: Dulce et decorum est/Pro patria mori.' (Owen: *Dulce et Decorum est*)
3   'Now the soldiers he smiled at are most of 'em dead.' (Sassoon: *The General*)
4   'As I pull the parapet's poppy/To stick behind my ear.' (Rosenberg: *Break of Day in the Trenches*)
5   'Age shall not weary them, nor the years condemn.' (Binyon: *For the Fallen*)
6   'Those that I fight I do not hate,/Those that I guard I do not love.' (Yeats: *An Irish Airman Foresees his Death*)
7   'O what made fatuous sunbeams toil/To break Earth's sleep at all?' (Owen: *Futility*)
8   'Not a drum was heard, not a funeral note/As his corse to the ramparts we hurried.' (Wolfe: *The Burial of Sir John Moore after Corunna*)
9   'If I should die, think only this of me...' (Brooke: *The Soldier*)

10 'The new men know not Beaucourt, but we are here – we know.' (Herbert: *Beaucourt Revisited*)
11 'Great Death has made all his for evermore.' (Sorley: *Sonnet*)
12 'Grinning as if it were all/An August Bank Holiday lark.' (Larkin: *MCMXIV*)
13 'Today I found in Mametz Wood/A certain cure for lust of blood.' (Graves: *A Dead Boche*)
14 'And strange-eyed constellations reign/His stars eternally.' (Hardy: *Drummer Hodge*)
15 'What passing-bells for these who die as cattle?' (Owen: *Anthem for Doomed Youth*)
16 'I died in hell –/They called it Passchendaele.' (Sassoon: *Memorial Tablet*)
17 'Its silence I hear and obey/That I may lose my way/And myself.' (Thomas: *Lights Out*)
18 'If I were fierce, and bald, and short of breath...' (Sassoon: *Base Details*)
19 'Beside my hate for one fat patriot/My hatred of the Kaiser is love true.' (Thomas: *This is no Case of Petty Right or Wrong*)
20 'Bloody saliva/Dribbles down his shapeless jacket.' (Read: *The Happy Warrior*)
(Numbers 8 and 14 were written before World War One.)

Friends and enemies (brief summaries)
1 Incompetent, dangerous, concerned with self-preservation.
2 No hatred for them, but must fight them to preserve England.
3 Dangerous liars responsible for filling young men's heads with nonsense.
4 Will be remembered as young and heroic for ever.
5 Represent the important things of life which survive and continue.

How do they do that?
1 Onomatopoeia ('stuttering'/'rattle')/alliteration of 'r' sound.
2 Simile (as we that are left...)/effectively simple diction.
3 Alliteration of 'n' sound/simile ('*like* hags')/metaphor ('cursed').
4 Alliteration of 'p'.
5 Metaphor ('Junkers').
6 Onomatopoeia ('flowing')/alliteration of 'fl'.
7 Metaphor: the whole of the poem is based on forest metaphor.
8 Alliteration of 's'/simile ('happy *as* her day').
9 Simile ('*like* a blind man's dreams').
10 Diction to characterise the different speakers.

Do you remember?
1 Choose from: *The Soldier*: *Anthem for Doomed Youth*; *Memorial Tablet*; *Sonnet* (Sorley).
2 Director of recruiting, 1915–16 (mentioned in *Memorial Tablet*).
3 A gas-shell (*Dulce et Decorum est*).
4 It is sweet and honourable to die for one's country.
5 Horace, a Latin poet.
6 Kiltartan.
7 Boche and Hun. (In *The Chances*, Owen uses 'Fritz'.)
8 A female poet/patriot attacked by Owen in *Dulce et Decorum est*.
9 Wilfred Owen.
10 Choose from: *Futility*; *Exposure*; *Strange Meeting*.
11 Excessively patriotic popular papers.
12 The typical British soldier.
13 Many people, but, by name (*Tommy*) Rudyard Kipling.
14 An aggressive patriot.
15 The two soldiers 'done for' by the general in Sassoon's poem, of that name.

Themes and poems

The following are merely hints and summaries of what you may have written:

1 In *The Soldier* (alive or dead) nature represents England; for Thomas natural things are real and eternal; in the two Rosenberg poems it represents brief peace (but still danger) and survival, respectively; *In Memoriam* compares flowers to soldiers: the Poppy Day idea.

2 Always a victim: of incompetent battle plans; of petty rules; of neglectful civilians.

3 Sleep always relates to death, but in different ways: eternal peace (*For the Fallen*); mysterious peace of dreams (*Lights Out*); both in *Strange Meeting*, a tormented dream that ends with a hope of peaceful sleep; fear of being reminded of the dead (*The Dug-Out*).

4 A changed, half-forgotten world; a dream of revenge on the Yellow Press and politicians; the continuation of what is truly important; eternal memory of the fallen.

5 Excitement; preserve English values; the squire nagged; self-fulfilment; patriotism.

Further reading

1 Owen obviously despises the attitudes in the newspaper. Those at home do not understand the soldiers. The secret is that 'England one by one had fled to France' and mostly England is now 'under France' – an odd echo of Rupert Brooke, but meant differently.

2 At first they are pleased to see the dead German by his gun. This changes to pity when they see the photograph of his girlfriend.

3 'He had a green face, spectacles, close-shaven hair; black blood was dripping from the nose and beard.'

4 Alcohol.

5 A season out of time, representing an England so old it stretches back before 'Merry England'.

Acknowledgements

Memorial Tablet p20, *Fight to a Finish* p24, *The General* p32, *Base Details* p32 and *The Dug-out* p50 by Siegfried Sassoon, reproduced by permission of George Sassoon. *For the Fallen* p18 by Laurence Binyon, reproduced by permission of Mrs Nicolete Gray and the Society of Authors, on behalf of the Laurence Binyon Estate. *The Happy Warrior* p44 by Herbert Read, reproduced by permission of David Higham Associates. *Judas and the Profiteer* p24 by Osbert Sitwell, reproduced by permission of David Higham Associates. *In Time of 'The Breaking of Nations'* p30 by Thomas Hardy, reproduced by permission of Macmillan. *An Irish Airman Foresees His Death* p54 by W B Yeats, reproduced by permission of A P Watt Ltd. *Beaucourt Revisited* p30 by A P Herbert, reproduced by permission of A P Watt Ltd on behalf of Crystal Hale and Jocelyn Herbert. *MCMXIV* p56 from *The Whitsun Weddings* by Philip Larkin, reproduced by permission of Faber & Faber Ltd.

■ Where to find the poems

(Page numbers in the **Text commentary** section)

■ Writing an examination essay

Take the following to heart

- *Carefully study each of the questions set on a particular text* Make sure you understand what they are asking for so that you select the one you know most about.
- *Answer the question* Obvious, isn't it? But bitter experience shows that many students fail because they do not actually answer the question that has been set.
- *Answer all the question* Again, obvious, but so many students spend all their time answering just part of a question and ignoring the rest. This prevents you gaining marks for the parts left out.

The question

1 Read and understand every word of it. If it asks you to compare (the similarities) and/or contrast (the differences) between characters or events, then that is what you must do.
2 Underline all the key words and phrases that mention characters, events and themes, and all instructions as to what to do, e.g. compare, contrast, outline, comment, give an account, write about, show how/what/where.
3 Now write a short list of the things you have to do, one item under the other. A typical question will only have between two and five items at most for you to cope with.

Planning your answer

1 Look at each of the points you have identified from the question. Think about what you are going to say about each. Much of it will be pretty obvious, but if you think of any good ideas, jot them down before you forget them.
2 Decide in what order you are going to deal with the question's major points. Number them in sequence.
3 So far you have done some concentrated, thoughtful reading and written down maybe fifteen to twenty words. You know roughly what you are going to say in response to the question and in what order – if you do not, you have time to give serious thought to trying one of the other questions.

Putting pen to paper

The first sentences are important. Try to summarise your response to the question so the examiner has some idea of how you are going to approach it. Do not say 'I am going to write about the character of Macbeth and show how evil he was' but instead write 'Macbeth was a weak-willed, vicious traitor. Totally dominated by his "fiend-like queen", he deserved the epitaph "this dead butcher" – or did he?' Jump straight into the essay, do not nibble at its extremities for a page and a half. High marks will be gained by the candidate who can show he or she has a mind engaged with the text. Your personal response is rewarded – provided you are answering the question!

As you write your essay *constantly refer back to your list of points* and make sure you are actually responding to them.

How long should it be?

There is no 'correct' length. What you must do is answer the question set, fully and sensitively, in the time allowed. Allocate time to each question according to the percentage of marks awarded for it.

How much quotation or paraphrase?

Use only that which is relevant and contributes to the quality and clarity of your answer. Padding is a waste of your time and gains not a single mark.